Recipe for Joy

Find your joy!

Robin Davis

Other Books by Robin Davis

Graeter's Ice Cream: An Irresistible History

North Market Cookbook

Infusions: Making Flavored Oils, Vinegars and Spirits

Wookiee Cookies: A Star Wars Cookbook

Recipe for Joy

A Stepmom's story
of finding faith,
following love,
and feeding
a family

Robin Davis

LOYOLAPRESS.
A JESUIT MINISTRY
Chicago

LOYOLA PRESS.
A JESUIT MINISTRY

3441 N. Ashland Avenue
Chicago, Illinois 60657
(800) 621-1008
www.loyolapress.com

Art Credits: Penelope Dullaghan, LokFung/istockphoto.com

ISBN-13: 978-0-8294-3795-9
ISBN-10: 0-8294-3795-9

Printed in the United States of America.
13 14 15 16 17 18 Bang 10 9 8 7 6 5 4 3 2 1

To Ken, Ben, Molly, and Sarah

Contents

Prologue
Our Lives Before

I took a last look in the mirror, eyeing the fashionable shag haircut and smoothing a few strands from my eyes. I threw my brown The Sak crocheted bag over my shoulder, smiling at the thought of the credit card inside bearing the name Susan Lamont, my alias, that waited to be used for the first time.

I almost skipped down the hall of the Victorian two-bedroom apartment that I shared with two other girls. My bedroom—a makeshift third bedroom—consisted of the second parlor, walled off with pocket doors from the first parlor that we used as a living room. It wasn't private, but it was darling. The apartment was on a tree-lined street in hipster Cole Valley, a world away from hippy Haight-Ashbury, a few blocks up.

As the fog rolled in, a nightly occurrence in San Francisco, I shouted good-bye to my roommates. Some days the fog was so thick that it never broke at all, blanketing the residents in a cold damp mist. Tonight, in this summer of 1997, it didn't bother me. Tonight the city had a special shine even through the fog. Tonight this city was mine.

I jumped behind the wheel of my shiny new black Jetta, expertly maneuvered it from its tight space between two other cars and threw it into first gear. I was headed to the theater district, to a new restaurant with owners as new to the restaurant business as I was to my job.

I was meeting a friend for dinner. But not just any dinner. I was now a restaurant critic at the *San Francisco Chronicle*. I would eat dinner incognito, my first of three visits over the course of the next few weeks, then write my opinion of what I ate. Thousands would read what I had to say and make dinner reservations based on my review.

As I drove to Indigo Restaurant, I thought what a long and sometimes speed bump-filled road it had been to get here.

I had chosen my career as my life, shutting the door on God and religion, and turning my back on any kind of long-term relationship years before. Being singularly driven to succeed, I believed, was something I could master, and far less messy than a life with a spouse and family. Marriage went against my philosophy that relationships had a useful lifespan, and when they were no longer useful, they should end.

Being married to my job was a decision my family didn't understand. When my oldest brother Rick asked when I would marry my current boyfriend du jour, I answered, "I don't have any plans to marry him or anyone else."

My brother, then married more than twenty years, answered, "Oh, yeah, I forgot that you live in the land of alternative lifestyles."

"Single" wasn't considered an alternative lifestyle in San Francisco, which was one of many reasons I loved the city so much. Career equaled identity to most of my friends. I knew I could thrive in such an environment.

My younger sister, who also had been married for many years, was less concerned with my getting married than my moving back to Ohio where I grew up and where she still lived.

"When I start having my kids," she pleaded, "I'll want you near me, near them."

"Dorothy," I explained as patiently as I could. "I will never, ever move back to Ohio."

In fact, I couldn't imagine ever leaving San Francisco. It was a magical place that had filled me with wonder from the first time I set foot in it to look at the California Culinary Academy. I was smitten by everything from the fingers of fog that reached across the headlands to the bustling crowds of people who seemed so smart and worldly.

I had worked hard to get where I finally was: leaving Ohio by myself to move to California, cashing in my 401K to go to cooking school, leaving my beloved San Francisco to move to Los Angeles to work for *Bon Appétit* magazine, then returning to the city by the bay to work as a part-time editorial assistant at the *Chronicle*. Now the paper was in the middle of nasty litigation with the woman who had been removed from the critic's job before it was given to me. But it was given to me. It was rightly mine.

Here I was, a small town girl from the Midwest, leading the ideal urban life in sexy San Francisco. Leave all this? I couldn't imagine what could possibly drive me to do something so crazy.

On that first night, I ordered pan-seared salmon with tomato fondue and pesto and instructed my friend to order roasted chicken atop okra risotto. We split smooth and silky lavender crème brulee for dessert. I paid careful attention to the service ("consistently good, and the staff seems to know the food well," I later wrote in the review) and the decor ("remodeled in sophisticated blue and white, the tiled bar outlined in pencil thin neon").

At the end of the night, I took careful notes and meticulously planned my next visits to this restaurant and others to fulfill my obligation of writing two reviews per week. I was positively giddy at the prospects.

This was the best night of my life.

At the same time, in a small suburb of Columbus, Ohio, Grace was sure she was having the worst night of her life. Finally, the kids were asleep, and her mother had reluctantly gone to bed. Grace sat across the kitchen table from her husband, the two of them just staring at each other.

Hours earlier, the phone had rung—a sound that in retrospect the couple would remember as a warning bell of something awful to come.

Ken had answered the phone in the bedroom. "Ken, this is Dr. Mathias. I need to talk to Grace. It's not good."

"I'm here, doctor," Grace said, having picked up the phone in the family room, as the kids played nearby under the watchful gaze of their grandmother. Grace sat on the floor next to the couch, nodding and taking careful notes in her precise handwriting. "Mmm, hmm. Yes. OK. Yes. I understand. I will," she said.

She hung up the phone, put her head in her hands, and cried. Ken knelt beside her, enveloping her in his arms. Her mother, Pat, stood from the chair where she was sitting, and Grace went to her next, seeking comfort even her mother couldn't give her.

"It's malignant," she said finally, watching five-year-old Ben and three-year-old twins Molly and Sarah who played with foam puzzles on the family room floor. Grace's world had just spun out of its orbit, yet the kids had no idea and happily worked to make the pieces fit.

The tumors were small, the doctor had said, but Grace needed to call the office on Monday so they could discuss their options.

After the call from Dr. Mathias, Ken and Grace packed the kids in their minivan along with Grace's mother and headed to City Center, a shopping mall in downtown Columbus. They walked the mall, trying to act normal, to not fall into despair.

Ken looked at other young families walking around, happy and carefree, and wondered, "Why us?" Much later, he would come to tell himself, "Why *not* us? Why are we so special that we should avoid life's pain?"

When Monday came, Grace made the appointment with Dr. Mathias for the next day. Meanwhile, Ken called St. Brigid of Kildare Church and asked to speak to a priest. He had been a practicing Catholic his whole life but had never felt such a desperate need for that faith to work somehow. When he told the priest his wife had been diagnosed with breast cancer, the pastor told him, "The first thing you have to remember is, it's not the end of the world."

It would be years before Ken understood that comment.

Still seeking solace, Ken went to the Little Professor Bookstore the same day on his lunch break, not far from where he worked as a civil engineer at a local architecture company. He picked up a book from the medical section, looking in the index for the words "breast cancer." He glanced around the bookstore to make sure no one was watching, then sat on a stool and read the relevant chapters. He couldn't bring himself to buy that book or any other—at least, not then—because that would have made the situation too real. He looked for statistics, answers to what the future held for them given the diagnosis, but ended up feeling confused and agitated.

At the appointment on Tuesday, Ken asked the doctor if there were any books he could read that would help him understand and give him a perspective of what was to come.

"Don't read any books," Dr. Mathias said. "Don't look at statistics because if you look at statistics, she shouldn't even have breast cancer. If you have any questions, come to me."

But what, Ken persisted, was the prognosis?

"We can't tell what the prognosis is. We can only make our decisions for the course of action based on what we know right now."

A lumpectomy wasn't the best option, he explained, because there were two tumors. They all agreed on a mastectomy and scheduled the surgery for Friday. Dr. Mathias removed the breast and the surrounding lymph nodes. Grace returned home a few days later with a drain in her chest.

After the surgery, the doctor thought the prognosis looked good because the tumors were small and the tests on the lymph nodes showed no signs of the cancer. After twelve weeks of healing from the surgery, Grace began a twelve-week regiment of chemotherapy, once every three weeks. They scheduled the chemo on Fridays so she would have the weekend to recover from the side effects: intense vomiting that would begin exactly eight hours after the drugs had dripped into her veins.

She lost weight from her tall, already lean frame, and lost her hair. When it started to fall out in clumps, she asked her husband to shave her head. Ken borrowed clippers from a neighbor, and they closed the door to their small downstairs bathroom. Shaking, Ken began to shave his wife's head.

What are we going to tell the kids? Ken thought, as he ran the clippers over and over his wife's head, her golden brown hair falling to the floor.

Grace put on a wig, and because they were both engineers, they gave the kids the scientific truth: The drugs Mom was taking went after all the fast-growing cells in her body because the "bad" cells that made her sick were the fast-growing kind. But hair was made of fast-growing cells, too, so the medicine would kill the hair. When she stopped taking the medicine and the bad cells were gone, her hair would grow back.

The kids listened, not fazed, or perhaps not understanding. Grace didn't parade around the house without a wig, scarves, or a denim ball cap. It wasn't often they actually saw her bald, and they didn't seem to notice.

But they did notice. Ben started kindergarten that fall and announced to his friend, Alex, that his mother was bald. At a soccer game one Saturday, Alex said, "Mrs. Heigel, Ben says you don't have any hair."

Grace leaned down and lifted her wig so he could peak at her smooth bald scalp. "It's true, Alex. But let's keep it our secret."

After the chemo, she was, for a time, cancer free.

Then in May of 1999, on a regular visit to her oncologist, the doctor found another tumor, again in the breast, but nearer the bone. She had outpatient surgery to remove the lump, and then another outpatient surgery to remove her ovaries to stop the body's production of estrogen that the doctors believed was feeding the tumors. Radiation started right away, for six weeks, every weekday.

Then, again, for more than a year, she appeared to be cancer free.

In the autumn of 2000, a regularly scheduled scan found spots on her vertebrae and kidney and in her lungs.

Grace was shocked. "I feel fine," she said. But the scans didn't lie. From the car, she called Ken. "They found spots," she said.

Ken went to the Internet, again looking for comfort. Instead he found words such as "metastatic" and "terminal," and phrases such as "zero survival rate." Still, he thought Grace could live for a while, maybe even for a few years. But Ken knew better than to ask the doctor how long she would live.

He called his parents. "Pray for Grace," he told his father. "Pray hard. The cancer has spread."

Grace started another round of chemotherapy that seemed gentler on her body, with fewer side effects. Her hair fell out again, but she didn't seem as sick.

Grace prayed for healing on a women's retreat at her church. "My hope is that my faith grows from this painful experience," she wrote in her journal. "I feel more confident that God will heal me, but I need to continue to ask for healing, even though I have so many people praying for me every day."

But by Christmas, the cancer in her bones collapsed her vertebrae, paralyzing her from the waist down and forcing her into a wheelchair. Ken's and Grace's families and friends drew closer. For a time, neighbors would help Ken carry Grace in her wheelchair to their second-floor bedroom every night. Then one of the neighbors went to friends, gathering donations so they could install a lift on the staircase to make transporting her easier. Parishioners at their church started regularly sending meals.

Grace was determined that year to go to the Easter vigil at St. Albert the Great in Dayton. Ken's brother-in-law Scot was coming into the church. Ken, Grace, Ben, Molly, and Sarah made the trip to Dayton, watching Scot, with Ken's dad as his sponsor, become confirmed. They returned home on Easter Sunday.

At 2:00 a.m., Grace woke Ken. "I can't breathe," she said. They rushed to the hospital. After a CAT scan, the ER doctor came in and told Ken that Grace had a blood clot in her lung.

"On a scale of 1 to 10, how bad is that?" Ken asked.

The doctor looked at him gravely. "It's a 10."

Ken felt his heart stop, a cold fist reaching into his chest. He left the ER to call his parents as the first rays of sun reached from the sky. "Mom?" he said. "I'm at the hospital with Grace. It's bad. It's really bad."

His parents were at his side when Grace's oncologist told him the plan. "We're going to give her a drug to dissolve the blood clot," Dr. Shapiro said. "It's risky, but we're still going to fight."

"You need to call St. Brigid," Beverly whispered to her son, after the doctor left them. Ken did so, asking for a priest. Then he called two friends from the parish, asking them to pray, too.

"We will," they assured him. "We'll call everyone. We'll pray."

Ken sent his own prayer heavenward: "Please, God. Not yet. Not yet."

After the doctors administered the drug, Monsignor Hendricks and Father Sizemore entered the darkened room, wearing their full black priestly attire and carrying a Bible. They anointed Grace with oil, praying for her to have courage and strength in her illness. Ken was comforted by the sacrament and felt a sense of peace.

Grace spent a week in intensive care, but the blood clot dissolved. She then moved to a rehabilitation house to regain her strength. She came home three weeks later, in time to celebrate Mother's Day.

She was too weak to navigate the stairs any longer, even with the lift, so Ken redecorated the first-floor home office, setting it up with a hospital bed, IV stands, and monitors. Ken's sister-in-law, Linda, a registered nurse, moved in to help with Grace's care.

But after a week at home, Ken again called for an ambulance. They were unable to manage Grace's pain. As she lay in the hospital recovering from a blood transfusion that gave her some relief, Dr. Shapiro told Ken she was no longer responding to treatment. There was nothing more they could do.

For the four years they had battled the disease, Ken had been strong, always looking outside himself to care for Grace and protect the children. At that moment, alone by the bedside of his sleeping wife, he cried.

He then moved Grace to Kobacker House, a hospice center. Ken would go to work in the morning, then take the kids to Kobacker in the afternoon to visit their mother. Some days, he couldn't bear for them to even go to school, so he would just take them to hospice all day.

"Why aren't the kids in school?" Grace would ask, confused in part from the powerful drugs meant to keep her comfortable, but also denying to herself the seriousness of her condition.

One day, Ken walked down the hall with Ben, to the end of the corridor. He sat him down in a chair, then knelt in front of him and put his hands on the tiny boy's knees. "There's nothing more the doctors can do for Mom, Ben," he said, his voice cracking. "She's going to go live with Jesus."

The little boy's sky blue eyes filled with tears. "Are you sure?"

Ken nodded. "There's nothing more they can do."

"Do the girls know yet?" Ben asked of his little sisters.

"Not yet," Ken said. That night, at home, he told them. The girls wanted to go outside to play, but first Ken sat them on the stairs, close together. "There's no more the doctors can do for Mom," he said, using the same words he had spoken to Ben. "She's going to go live with Jesus."

They looked at him, not quite understanding, and anxious to get outside with their friends. "OK," they said.

Too tired to explain more, he let them go.

The next day the three children sat at the kitchen table, coloring and talking in hushed tones, as their Aunt Kim, Ken's sister, washed dishes nearby. Suddenly, Molly began to wail. "No, no!" she cried.

Kim went to her, clutching the girl in her arms. Molly had risen from her seat and stood beside the chair, clinging to the edge of the kitchen table, shaking violently. "Mom is NOT going to die!"

That day at Kobacker, the doctors discussed with Ken the option of Grace coming home to die. The thought tormented him. He wanted her to die with dignity and in the most comfort possible, but he worried how the children would react to the room, to the whole house, if she died there.

As he fell asleep that night, wrapped tightly in a fetal position, Ken felt God come to him. He felt a physical presence wrapping itself around him, holding him tight. At that moment, he turned the battle over to God.

"Your will be done," he thought as he faded to sleep. He slept, and awoke in a peace he hadn't felt in months. He went to Kobacker that day, carrying the same calmness, knowing God would carry him through whatever happened. When he walked into Grace's room, she was sitting up, her head wrapped in a scarf. She looked at Ken and smiled.

"I want to go home," she said. She came home the next day.

A few days later, Ken sent the kids to school as he always did, trying to keep their world as normal as possible for as long as he could. When Linda, Ken's sister-in-law who had moved in to help with her care, checked Grace's vital signs that morning, she told Ken this would be the day, Grace's last. He went back to school and brought the children home.

At 3:10 that afternoon, surrounded by her mother and father, her husband, Linda, a priest, and her nine-year-old son, Grace died.

Ben looked at her still body, holding on to her cold hand, and asked, "Is she with Jesus now?"

His father said, "She is." Ben smiled.

Earlier in the week, Ken's parents had gone to buy the funeral plots, and as they left, Linda told them, "Buy three." Everyone stopped and looked at her.

"You may get married again," she said to Ken.

"Absolutely, positively, I am never getting married again."

"Oh, you better buy three," she said. So they did.

After Grace died, Ken went to pick out the headstone, taking Ben, Molly, and Sarah and two of their cousins, Michael and Katie. He wanted something black and shiny, but let the kids choose the actual stone. They wanted funny inscriptions and drawings, Disney characters or wedding rings, but in the end, they chose something simpler: an outline of the University of Dayton chapel, which her gravesite overlooked on a hilltop not far from campus.

At the funeral, Ken eulogized his wife of twelve years. "Her determination showed in everything she did. She always had a set of goals."

He looked out at the hundreds of mourners packing St. Brigid of Kildare. "As for goals, Grace and I learned that God has his set of goals, too. This is part of his plan. God has put us in place and around people to give us strength and courage to accept life and death."

He then focused on Ben, Molly, and Sarah, who looked so small in the first pew of the church. "His plan continues," Ken said, now speaking only to the three of them. "Grace is still part of that plan. This is not the end of life, but the beginning of new life, Grace's eternal life. She is going to be with us wherever we go.

"Hopefully, we have learned something from Grace's journey. For me, Grace has given me the strength to accept. For all of us, Grace has given us the ability to pray to God for strength and thankfulness."

He took a deep breath and continued. "There is no more wheel-chair, no more tests, no more treatment, no more doctor appointments. Grace has won the battle. She is a survivor. She has been healed."

Later, after the graveside service, the family walked away, leaving behind the black headstone, engraved with the silhouette of the chapel and inscribed: Grace Kelleher Heigel, born November 28, 1965, died June 4, 2001. Next to that was Ken's name followed by his birth date. And next to Ken's name was a blank space, smooth and unmarked, an afterthought, a just-in-case.

Someday—I hope not too soon—it will be my name in that space on that shiny black gravestone.

This is the story of how someone who turned her back on God found her way back when she didn't even know she was lost. It is the story of how I answered his call and did what I swore I never would do, how I became the wife to Ken and the mom-on-earth to Ben, Molly, and Sarah, and how my reluctant devotion gave me the gift of grace.

1

The Toast

Here's a gesture we all know: glasses clinking together, a ceremonial sip, smiles, and good wishes. The concept of the toast may be associated with celebrations, but its history is a bit darker.

Legend has it that the ritual came about in ancient Greece as a way for the host to prove he was not poisoning his guest, which at the time was a popular way of disposing of one's enemies. The host would pour two glasses from the same vessel and take the first sip. Upon seeing that the host did not become ill, the other could then drink safely.

Calling the tradition a "toast" supposedly came hundreds of years later when it became customary to place a small piece of burnt bread in each cup of wine, perhaps to obscure the bad taste of the beverage.

Today, there are few more universal gestures than the raising of a glass in honor of everything from birthdays to weddings.

As a toddler, my sister's second child, Freddie, was so fond of toasting that he liked to use it daily—and it didn't have to be a glass he raised. He would clink chicken nuggets or sippy cups or Pop Tarts, and say, "Cheers!" with pure delight. And maybe the little boy was right to use the toast so freely and joyfully. There is, after all, much to celebrate from birthdays and weddings to everyday miracles.

My wedding day was the kind of day Disney advertises: perfect spring weather, neither too hot nor too cold, and nothing but blue cloudless skies. The grass was luscious and green after days of rain, every tree and shrub bursting open in pinks and purples and whites. Forsythia blazed yellow, and magnolias ostentatiously presented their showy, fist-sized flowers.

But what I remember most about that day was my unwavering joy. I didn't have a moment of nervousness or a single second of second thoughts. From the time I sat at the spa in the early morning having my hair styled and my makeup applied to the late evening hours when my husband and I left our house after the after-party we threw for our out-of-town guests, I was nothing but happy.

I was no Disney princess bride, marrying my college sweetheart in a ball gown as big as a baked Alaska. Our wedding was a more subdued event, held at St. Brigid of Kildare Church at 10:30 in the morning, followed by a brunch reception at the same country club where my groom and I had had our second date.

At first, I had wanted a smaller wedding, no country club affair. But when we made the list of family who absolutely had to be invited, already there were nearly one hundred names. We played with the idea of a destination wedding—just us, on a beach or maybe a cruise. We toyed with the idea of inviting friends over to the house for an engagement party only to spring on them that we were actually getting married that day, right then.

In the end, we took a more traditional route, for the sake of the kids.

Had it just been Ken and me, we probably would have been happy with a small private ceremony. But this wedding wasn't just about the two of us. It was about forming a family. We wanted Ben, Molly, and Sarah to know that this was a big deal and the happiest of occasions, coming nearly three years after the saddest of days. Having the wedding at St. Brigid closed the circle from Grace's death and burial to our marriage and new life together, a sign to us of God's grace.

We involved the children in every step. Ben sang during the ceremony in his beautiful twelve-year-old voice. Molly and Sarah were my junior bridesmaids, going with me to the salon in the morning to have their hair and nails done, too. We even chose a cake geared toward children, a whimsical topsy-turvy concoction with sparklers shooting out of the top.

We took great care to invite families with children who were close friends to Ben, Molly, and Sarah. If this was a family affair, they should have guests of their own. Of the 150 guests, about a third were children, so we set up a separate buffet for them at the reception with kid-friendly foods such as chicken fingers, fries, and bite-size pieces of fruit.

Before we ate, my sister, who was my matron of honor, offered a toast.

"There were three things Robin told me she would never do," Dorothy said, pausing dramatically after each one.

"She would never join an organized religion.

"She would never move back to Ohio.

"And she would never ever get married."

There was one other of my "nevers" that my sister tactfully left off the list: I had said that I would never have children.

The crowd roared with laughter as I stood there, a newly confirmed Catholic, newly married, and now living in a suburb of Ohio's state capital. And a new mother, too, or at least a stepmother.

That this day had occurred was nothing short of a miracle, really. Each step that had led me here was a gift of grace, though I could hardly have seen them as such at the time.

Almost three years earlier, I surveyed my studio apartment one last time. It was spacious by San Francisco standards and looked even more so now that it was empty. The hardwood floors of the main area were dull and scratched. The kitchen gleamed off-white, with built-in cupboards inlaid with glass panels, and enough space on the black and white tiled floor for a small table, a luxury most studios didn't offer.

The tree outside sported the very last of its amazing poinsettia flowers, blooming all the way to my second floor window. My friends who garden say poinsettias don't grow into trees, but this one did behind my apartment at 17th and Church streets, as though someone had transplanted the potted Christmas plant into the backyard soil years ago and forgotten about it. Yet it had grown into something magnificent, in spite of the neglect.

Beyond the tree sat Mission High School, where almost every night except in the most inclement weather, a group of men, mostly Latino, started a pick-up game of soccer. Alongside the school ran the tracks for the J-Church MUNI line. Each day the first train woke me at 5:00 a.m. and said its last goodnight at 1:00 a.m. I never needed an alarm clock when I lived here.

All my furniture was loaded onto a moving truck. This was it: the final good-bye. I was leaving the city that I'd sworn I would never leave and moving back to Ohio, to which I'd sworn I would never return.

My nerves felt raw and on the surface of my skin now, as though I were wrapped in barbed wire, imprisoned and untouchable. I simply couldn't stay here any more.

I had said as much to my boss a few months earlier.

"I just can't do this anymore." "This" was restaurant criticism. "This" was food writing. But mostly "this" was being away from my simultaneously shrinking and growing family. At age thirty-six, suddenly I was the oldest generation. I just couldn't bear being away from the hope of the newest generation, thousands of miles away.

I no longer wanted to be the glamorous aunt who lived on the West Coast and came to visit every few years. I wanted to be the aunt my newborn nephew saw every day.

I hungered for peace and quiet. I longed for a calmer existence that didn't involve battling for parking spaces every night, being on an endless search for new restaurants, and living and breathing for work. I just wanted a break.

But I was turning my back on everything I had worked so hard for. No one was more confused by my feelings than I. The events of the past year had changed everything, forcing me to revisit what my life was and what I wanted it to be.

Sometimes I say that it started with a phone call from my father, but cracks had been appearing in the veneer of my perfect life for years.

As a critic, every night was spent at a restaurant, and every day was spent writing about those restaurants. When the glamour and newness of the job wore off, the reality set in: Not all the restaurants were good, but I still had to write about them. While on my meanest day, I might fantasize about writing a scathing review of an unworthy restaurant, I didn't really have the stomach for it. I'd been to cooking school, I'd worked in restaurants, and I knew how hard it was to put out good food every night. When the time came to write the negative—or even ho-hum—review, I couldn't put the owner's or chef's face out of my mind.

Dining out every night definitely put a damper on my love life, too. I may not have wanted to get married, but men seemed to find even dating a restaurant critic unpalatable. Not only did they not get to choose where we would go for dinner, they couldn't even select what to order. I carefully scripted every meal. As progressive as San Francisco was, the men I dated quickly tired of my dedication to the job.

The temporariness of my lifestyle grew stale. Nothing was permanent, nothing lasted. I couldn't have a favorite restaurant or a favorite meal because I was on to the newest restaurant or the next great food trend. My worth came only from my last review or my latest story, which ended up on the bottom of litter boxes and bird cages within hours of being printed.

This meticulously detailed life I had created seemed to be lacking something. But I couldn't pinpoint what it was.

In the spring of 2000, my father called, setting off a chain of events that forced me to reconsider what I held dear. Later, I would realize that the call was God's first whisper telling me to return to him. At least, it was the first whisper I chose to hear.

I had always been looking for God, seeking a higher power in one form or another. In the innocence of youth, I had an overwhelming belief, a feeling deep in my heart that some kind of greater being was watching over me.

When I was eight or so, I became worried about the end of the world. I would cry myself to sleep some nights wondering if all of it would come to an end in a fireball and imagining the pain of burning up in it.

Years later, a therapist would tell me that I probably felt that my home life wasn't stable, that I was afraid that *my* world—not necessarily the whole world—was ending. But that wasn't completely right. There was some instability in my parents' relationship. But there was never a threat of violence or divorce or job loss, things that would have changed the world I lived in. I believe I had a real fear that I would not be able to find—or understand or be accepted by—God, whoever God was.

As a family, we rarely went to church. I saw photos of my oldest brothers serving as altar boys, but it seemed that as the brood grew, the need—or was it the desire? the resolve?—to attend church dwindled. I was the fourth of five children, following three boys ranging in age from eighteen months to nine years. Five years after me came my sister. My parents had a houseful.

They both had been raised in the Episcopal tradition. Occasionally, they would muster the effort to get us to the Episcopal church near the Air Force base where my father worked. But as I grew older, my family's regular worship attendance at the Episcopal church transitioned into attendance at Sunday school, but only sometimes and at any nearby Protestant church.

One early summer Sunday, my father, wearing a ratty undershirt and jeans, dropped off my brother, sister, and me at a Lutheran church close to our house. We had attended this church more off than on for the past year or so. My oldest brothers, now well into their teens, seemed spared such events.

The three of us walked into the breezeway that worked as the main entrance and headed to the right, to where Sunday school normally was held, just a large room partitioned with moving walls, tables and folding chairs. But on this sunny morning, with humidity already building in typical midwestern fashion, the room was empty. Mark, Dorothy, and I walked back to the breezeway, but my father was already gone, having promised to return in an hour or so, when most people arrived for church services. My parents wouldn't come to the services, but thought, I guess, that if the three of us at least went to Sunday school that would be something.

With nothing to do but wait, we wandered into the church to discover that the worship service had already begun. As we opened the door, heads turned to look at us. I remember it as a ten-year-old would: The whole service stopped and the entire congregation turned to stare at the people who would dare come so late to church. In reality, it was more likely a few wondering eyes and maybe a kindly woman in the back row motioning for us to come in and sit. I was no less mortified. But we had no choice, so we went in and sat uncomfortably through the service, rushing out as soon as it was over to jump into our Dad's waiting car. It turned out that the Sunday school and service schedule had changed for the summer, but being sporadic attendees, we hadn't known.

My brother and I never went back to that church, I think because we complained so much to our parents about our embarrassment. But years later, when my oldest brothers had moved out of the house and I was entrenched in high school, my parents would go to this Lutheran church with my sister every Sunday. Maybe with just one child it wasn't so hard to navigate getting to church regularly. But I think my own faith journey may have played a part in their decision as well.

"Hi, Rob," my father said when he called me in San Francisco that afternoon in 2000, his voice thick.

My father didn't call often; we hadn't been close for most of my adult life. While my siblings nudged me to return to Ohio or to settle down, my father didn't seem to care one way or the other. It was my life, he would say, and I truly believed that's what he meant. Still, it stung a little. What daughter doesn't want her father's love and attention?

"I got the results from the biopsy," he said. He cleared his throat. "It's pancreatic cancer."

I wasn't familiar with pancreatic cancer. I didn't know that he was essentially telling me he'd been given a death sentence.

"But the doctor feels good about it," Dad said, in the most cheerful voice this somber man could muster. "There was no cancer in the lymph nodes. That's a positive sign."

Later, I researched pancreatic cancer, and was horrified by what I found. Fewer than 10 percent of those diagnosed with it live more than a year.

I searched my soul in those first few weeks after his phone call, asking myself about my relationship with him. Maybe he was nonchalant about our separation. Maybe he really didn't care. But how did I feel? What did I want?

On the most basic level, I wanted my father to know I loved him, and I believed the best way to show it was to be with him as often as I could. I flew to Dayton that summer when he started chemotherapy and radiation. For a week, I lived in the house he shared with my stepmother, whom he had married years after my mother died.

Ann was a kind woman, but I thought it odd that my father, a brilliant man, had not wanted someone more intellectually challenging. My mother had been smart and charming and witty. And, as an alcoholic, she was quite challenging in other ways.

My mother had been a widow at age twenty-four. She had married her college sweetheart who was a pilot in the Air Force. They were wildly in love. But when his plane crashed, she was left with a broken heart and two young sons.

She told me stories of how hard it had been to be young and essentially single in the late 1950s. After a time, married friends stopped inviting her to parties because she was the only one who wasn't married. Working to support her two little boys was difficult, too. So she did the only the thing she could do. She got married.

To me, my mother and father had never seemed close to one another. Growing up, I often thought, *If this is marriage, then I don't get it.*

Maybe after my mother died, my father decided he wanted something simpler, less chaotic. That's what he got: a simple life with a woman who cared a great deal about appearances and who positively doted on him.

During the week I spent with Dad, I took him to and from the hospital every day for his treatments. I wanted to give Ann a break; I knew my father could be challenging in his own right. But I also wanted to try to build bridges with him, to catch up on lost time, and maybe have the close relationship with him that had seemed so elusive.

We did spend quality time together. I met the nurses and other patients going through treatment. He boasted to them that I was his daughter, the "chef and writer."

I tried to get him to eat, something I'm typically good at. The disease and its treatment caused weight to just melt off him, dropping him to a mere 135 pounds at its lowest from his normal already lean 160. I made what I remembered were his favorite meals when I was growing up: sausages and warm German potato salad; steaks and leaf lettuce salad with a sizzling bacon dressing; lasagna with layers of meat sauce and cheese. He ate, but never much. The drugs changed the way things tasted, he said.

One hot evening after I'd cleaned up the dishes and Ann had gone to visit her mother, I asked my dad about my mom. How had they met? He answered with an openness I'd never seen in him.

He had been in love with my mother since they met during college. But she had always been Dick's girl. A respectable time after Dick died, Dad asked her to marry him. My mother turned him down. He said he asked her several more times over the years. Finally she relented.

It was what I had always suspected: He had married for love, and she married because it was practical—which was ironic because my mother had been the romantic and my father, the scientist, seemed all logic.

When he finished the story, I renewed my vow to never get married. I never wanted to settle. I had watched my parents through wordless meals. I had watched their anger toward each other bubble up, especially when they were drinking.

My dad had plenty to be angry about. He married my mother because he loved her, and he hoped that eventually she would love him, too, despite her grief. Instead, she did what was expected of her: bore him three children and tended house. But mostly she retreated into her alcoholic haze, into her own world, where she wasn't available emotionally to him or anyone else.

At the end of the week I spent with him at his home that summer, I packed the rental car to go to the airport. He stood on the front walk, watching me go. When I said good-bye, his eyes welled with tears, and he held me tightly if only for a moment. We looked at each other, wondering if it would be the last time we would see one another.

It wasn't. I returned in the fall for his retirement from the University of Dayton, where I had been able to go tuition free because he worked there as a research chemist after he retired from the Air Force. UD held many memories for me, but most were buried under years of neglect. On the day of my father's retirement, I walked the campus, remembering the paths and the buildings, and finally sat for a while in the chapel.

The first Mass I ever attended was with my best friend, Maria, in the UD chapel. Maria was a devout Catholic and something of a feminist. She believed women should be allowed to be priests, but she also believed strongly in the Catholic Church.

She answered all my questions about the Mass: why we knelt, why we stood, why we made small crosses on our eyes, lips, and hearts before the reading of the Gospel. I loved it—the ritual, the meaning, the centuries of tradition.

It was, of course, a more contemporary Mass geared toward college students, with lively music and an upbeat atmosphere. And it was packed with students, my peers. These were people who chose to go to Mass without being forced by parents or without being Jesus freaks, something I'm sure we were called in high school when I was active in the Fellowship of Christian Athletes. They were just "normal" students, enjoying all the joys of college life, including partying. Yet here they were, so many, without obligation, choosing to go to Mass.

Through Maria, I joined Campus Ministry, sort of a college version of high school youth group. And as in high school, I found my niche with these faith-based people. We had retreats twice a year, and I became one of the leaders. I loved the sense of community the church and campus ministry brought me.

But I was also a perpetual outsider because I wasn't Catholic. I could participate in everything except the Eucharist. No one talked to me about becoming a Catholic, and I didn't ask. I'm not sure it even occurred to me that an adult could become Catholic. It was something you were born into or not. And I was not.

Maybe it was the feelings of exclusion that eventually made me drift away from the group and allowed me to set my sights on a bad relationship. I still longed to fit in completely, somewhere, with someone. Maybe with this much older man I could feel loved, overlooking his gambling problem, his streaks of cruelty. As I invested in this relationship, all it really did was isolate me further from the campus community, my friends, and my faith.

And then my mother died, and I was lost.

Six months after my father's retirement from UD, on the night before I was to leave for New York to attend the glamorous James Beard Awards given to the year's top chefs and food writers (one of which I had won the previous year), my father was rushed to the hospital for emergency surgery to remove a growth from his abdomen.

I cancelled my trip and instead flew to his bedside, but not without a laptop so I could finish a story I was working on. Deadlines couldn't be missed just because someone was sick, no matter how grave.

And it was grave, his doctor told us, though I had made her wait while I whipped out the last few sentences on my piece and finally hit "send" on a story I no longer even remember. The tumor wasn't cancerous, Dr. Barney said, but his body had been ravaged by the cancer treatment and its side effects.

For a week, my siblings and I held a vigil in the intensive care unit, a hallway that surrounded a series of doors, a different patient behind each one. We sat and slept on benches and chairs outside his room where he lay in a medically induced coma. His bed inflated and deflated to keep his body moving to prevent bed sores, and the ventilator kept his breathing regular. He was surrounded by an array of machines that measured oxygen levels and blood pressure and heart beats.

As stressful as it was, my four siblings and I felt a sort of childlike joy being together again. We hadn't all been in the same room in years. Now, through less-than-perfect circumstances, we were forced to be together.

We gathered and separated throughout each day. Rick, who had been a cameraman for a local television news station before moving to St. Louis and starting a career in computer science, liked to make his way down the IC corridor, sitting among families, listening quietly, then reporting back to us.

"Two down? That's a gunshot victim," he said of the family two doors away from us. "The one right next to us? He had a heart attack."

Mark, who now lived in Janesville, Wisconsin, would wander to other wards in the hospital or to the cafeteria for coffee.

Scott, the only one of us who still lived in Dayton, was happy to go out and gather food, bringing in favorites I hadn't enjoyed in years: Marion's Pizza with its rabbit-pellet like sausage, cheesesteaks from Submarine House, Killer Brownies from Dorothy Lane Market.

Dorothy and I mostly stayed right where we were, occasionally going into Dad's room to hold his hand or talk to him, though we knew he was unable to respond. My sister was almost seven months pregnant with her first child. We talked about the baby, her excitement and fears, how she hoped Dad would live to meet it. And she used every opportunity to remind me she wanted me near the baby as it was growing up.

As a diversion from the day-to-day intensity, I checked in frequently with the *Chronicle*, feeling the pull between my real life and this past life.

Ann would pop in once a day, usually midafternoon. She always looked impeccable, with her hair and nails just done, wanting, I suppose, to look beautiful for her husband if he happened to regain consciousness. She always hoped to catch the doctor, to hear the daily update of Dad's condition. The five of us had learned early on that intensive care doctors don't keep regular hours, and if you wanted a status report, you'd better be there all day.

When she would miss the doctor, she would totter away on her high heels, telling us of an errand she needed to run or something she had to do at the house. Clearly keeping the house running, their lives in order, was critical to her, to maintain the appearance, and the hope, that he was going to return home.

None of the other patients stayed very long in intensive care. Most moved to another ward as the patient's condition improved. But Dad's condition neither improved nor deteriorated. At the end of the week, he was no better or worse than he had been at the beginning. Dr. Barney told us his condition was day to day, hour to hour.

One by one, we each had to return to our lives, to our jobs. After a week, only Dorothy and Scott remained close enough to visit him each day.

I reluctantly returned to San Francisco, but checked in with my sister several times a day. We found ourselves constantly analyzing his stats, as though we were experts: His oxygen level was good but his kidney secretions were down. His blood pressure was erratic, but his breathing was stable.

Every day we wondered if this was the day he would die or improve. And every day, for six weeks, he did neither.

Toward the end of May, I was scheduled to fly to Florence to do a story on vacation cooking schools in Italy for the *Chronicle's* travel section. I was torn. Dad was still in intensive care, still in a coma. Did I dare leave?

"Go," Dorothy told me. "His condition hasn't changed in six weeks."

I went, taking a cell phone just in case. I stopped in London for a few days to visit a friend who had relocated there from San Francisco, then flew on to Rome and drove to Florence. I had settled into an early dinner at a wine bar across the street from my hotel when my cell phone rang.

"Dad's taken a turn for the worse," Dorothy said. "I don't expect you to come home. But I knew you'd want to know."

I left the restaurant, holding up a finger to my waiter, the universal sign for "just a minute; I have to take this." I paced in the narrow street, jumping onto the curb whenever a car rushed by, clutching the phone to my ear. "How bad is it?"

"All his organs are failing, Robin," she said, resigned more than tearful.

"How long does he have then?"

"The thing is, he's on life support with the ventilator and everything. We have to remove him from life support. His living will says that Ann and the five of us have to be in agreement."

I paused. The setting sun was still bright, casting a golden light on this ancient city, thousands of miles from my home and my dying father. Could I stay here in Florence and dutifully continue my research for this story, waiting for the phone call telling me it was over? What could I do in Dayton, really? He wouldn't even know I was there.

But I would know. Forever, I would know that I was the girl who didn't do everything she could to say one last good-bye to her father, to tell him she loved him and to hold his hand as he left this life.

"I'm coming home," I said. "Don't remove him from life support until I get there."

I battled my way back to Rome by car on the crowded Italian freeways, and then found flights one at a time, first to Chicago, then to Dayton.

And I prayed. For the first time in more than a decade, I prayed. It was a whisper, only in my head, but a prayer nonetheless. "God, if I'm supposed to get there before he dies, let it happen. And if it's not meant to be, give me the strength to be okay with it."

I arrived at the hospital twenty-four hours later, sleepless and bleary-eyed, the last of his children to make it to his bedside. I pulled a chair up to his bed and finally dozed. At about six in the morning, I awoke when his family doctor came in the room. Dr. Ljungren touched my father's arm and said, "I'm so sorry, Ken."

He looked at me with kind eyes. "I'm sorry." I watched him walk out the door and knew this really was the end for my father. A lump formed in my throat.

Dr. Barney gathered us together a little while later. "You awake, world traveler?" she asked me. I nodded. She explained they would stop giving him heart medication and regulating his blood pressure. But they would keep the morphine steady so he would not feel any pain. The ventilator would stay. Despite the colloquialism, there was, in fact, no real "plug" to pull.

We gathered around his bedside, trying to take in the moment and watch him, but found ourselves watching the monitors instead.

A nurse stuck her head in. "Do you need a priest or a minister?" she asked. "Is there anyone we can call?" We shook our heads. There had been so little religion in our home when we were growing up. None of us could ask for it now.

Minutes ticked by, and we watched his heart rate fluctuate, his blood pressure plummet, then climb. "This could take hours," Mark whispered after about an hour, traumatized at the prospect of watching his father struggle like this.

Dorothy started to cry. "No," she said. She leaned in close to Dad, put her hand on his chest and said, "It's OK, Dad. We're here. We're all here. It's OK. It's OK for you to go."

And just like that, he died.

In the weeks that followed his funeral, I tried to get back my old life in San Francisco, but nothing felt right. The sun was too bright. People were too cheerful. Life kept going, but mine seemed to have stopped. I was prone to bouts of crying at the office, in coffee shops, and, more than once, at restaurants I was reviewing.

My whisper-prayers, the ones I had started on the plane back from Italy, continued. I would lie on my hardwood floor, outstretched with my face down and hands over my head, tears dripping from my cheeks.

"Please. Please. Please."

It was all I could manage. This pain was so great. This hole in my heart was so big. I was thirty-six and an orphan. Would I ever be complete? Would this agony ever stop?

"Please. Please. Please."

The whispers started to be answered, first in the form of a new life: my nephew. With Josh's birth, happiness returned to my life in bits and pieces. When I held him, I felt hope. When I watched him sleep, I felt peace, my weeping soul silenced, at least for a few moments.

I spent Thanksgiving that year in Columbus with my sister, her husband, and little Josh. I spent my days cooking for the holiday and for Josh's baptism, which Dorothy had postponed until I could be there. And I spent every moment I could holding the baby, who even at four months seemed full of personality.

Being around Josh did not make me long for a child of my own. I knew I was too selfish to be a good mother. But I did long to be part of this child's life. I would sit in an overstuffed chair with my feet on the ottoman and lay him on my legs facing me. I would make faces at him if he was awake or just watch him if he was asleep. And I would tell him over and over how much I loved him.

On my return flight to San Francisco, a freak snowstorm blew through the Midwest, grounding me in Chicago for several hours. When I checked in with the office, my boss gave me bad news: The *Chronicle* was accepting buyouts.

Was it a sign? In the months and years that followed, I took it as such. Maybe I wasn't supposed to return to San Francisco. Maybe I was supposed to stay in Columbus. My whispering to God continued. "If you want me to move to Columbus, give me a sign."

If there was a sign, it was only that my thoughts of accepting the buyout persisted. No thunderous clap of foreboding came from the skies. No stranger on the street whispered in my ear that I should remain on the West Coast.

By the time I awoke the next morning, I knew I was going to do it. I was quitting my glamorous job in my fabulous city and moving "home." I felt both terrified and exhilarated.

"Make someone stop me if you don't want me to do this," I whisper-prayed.

At work, I asked for a meeting with my boss, Miriam. She was like a mother to me and the rest of the department. I knew leaving the *Chronicle* would be bittersweet. These people had been my family for the past several years. Now I wanted to leave to be with my real family.

"I want to take the buyout," I told her.

Miriam's eyes got big. She looked confused.

"I want to be near my sister."

Her eyes filled with tears. She nodded.

No one tried to talk me out of the decision. Instead, in the next days Miriam and the executive food editor, Michael, convinced me not to take a buyout, but worked out a six-month sabbatical instead. I had weeks of vacation coming to me. I could use that for some of the time, keep my health insurance, and still write freelance stories for the paper. They didn't want me to cut ties completely. They didn't believe, not really, that I'd be gone for more than six months.

But Miriam's husband had a premonition.

"You're going to fall in love and get married," he said at my going-away party at Michael's house. Everyone howled with laughter, and I was the loudest.

One thing I was *not* doing was moving to Columbus to find a new crop of men. I thought that I was actually through with dating. My plan was to live a quasi-celibate life, focusing on my sister and Josh, figuring out my next step.

Here I was closing the door on a chapter of my life and starting something new. I drove across the country with Laura, my friend from college who had moved to the Bay Area. She had, in fact, driven to California with me when I originally moved out thirteen years before. We took the same route back, stopping at a few of the same places: the artsy shops in Flagstaff, Arizona, and The Big Texan in Amarillo, Texas, where if you eat a 64-ounce steak with all the trimmings within an hour, you get to stay in the adjoining hotel for free. (We paid for our room.)

We made new stops, too, including an Indian reservation outside Palm Springs where I picked up a sage stick to burn in my new home so I could start my new life free of any lingering negative spirits. I didn't necessarily believe it would work, but I was making such a big move, I thought I could use any help, real or imagined, I could get.

I pulled into the driveway of my new address, a two-bedroom townhouse just blocks away from my sister, late one evening in February. It was bitterly cold and dark, so unappealing.

My sister had let the movers in days before, so the space was filled with boxes of my stuff. I walked through each room, from the galley kitchen through the dining room and living room. Up the wooden staircase past the tiny bathroom with forest green tile, a small bedroom I would use as an office, and finally my bedroom with a built-in window seat that overlooked King Avenue.

This was my new home, my new life. My stomach felt as if I had swallowed stones.

What have I done? I wondered.

I had been living in Columbus for about a month, picking up freelance stories for the *Columbus Dispatch* and *Ohio Magazine*, and working part-time as a buyer at a local gourmet cookware/grocery store, when my sister recommended an evening out.

"Let's go to a UD alumni dinner," she suggested.

Our alma mater had an active alumni association in Columbus. I'd kept in touch with virtually no one, save Laura, when I left Ohio years ago.

"I'll go, but I won't know anyone," I told her.

We were some of the first people at the event, but in the lobby of the restaurant was a man with close-cropped wavy dark hair and sparkly green eyes who looked vaguely familiar.

"Hi. I'm Ken Heigel."

"I'm Robin. This is my sister, Dorothy," I said. "You look familiar."

"I graduated in '87."

"Me, too."

He had a degree in engineering while I had majored in English, so we definitely hadn't crossed paths in classes.

"I used to take photos for the *Flyer News*," he said.

I had been the sports editor for the university's newspaper my senior year, but that's when he had co-oped, working one semester, taking classes the next.

At dinner, we sat across from each other at a long table filled with other alumni, none of whom I knew. We continued to chat, about work and about wine. He was fascinated by my previous job and asked lots of questions. We shared a pleasant familiarity right from the beginning.

At one point, he mentioned children at home being watched by their grandmother. I stole a quick glance at his left hand. No ring. Must be divorced, I thought.

"Where did you live at UD?" he asked after the appetizers had been cleared.

"Marycrest, Campus South, then on Brown Street my junior and senior year."

"Where on Brown Street?"

"On the corner, across the street from Holy Angels."

"Did you know Maria Carroll? I think she lived near there."

"Maria? She was my best friend in college. We lived together on Brown Street."

Ken's face got soft. He looked down and kind of smiled.

"When my wife was sick—she had breast cancer—Maria wrote her letters, telling her about when her mother had breast cancer. Grace and Maria never met, but the letters meant a lot to her."

That sounded like the Maria I remembered: an English major, like me, who wrote long letters at Christmas. In the years right after our graduation, those letters had detailed her mother's fight with breast cancer. I had long since lost touch with her, as I had with just about everyone else from my past life.

I didn't say anything.

"My wife died almost a year ago." As it turned out, Grace had died exactly four days after my father died.

From that moment, it was as if there was no one else in the room. I listened to him talk about Grace and her illness and his three kids. I told him about my dad and his fight with another cancer. We commiserated about the big changes life sometimes throws at you.

When the desserts were cleared and it was time to go, I did something I had never done before: I gave him my phone number. As I handed it to him, I felt a charge, almost like a static shock, a surge of energy.

When my sister and I left the restaurant, I turned and looked back, watching him walk to his car. I caught my sister's eye as I turned back around. She raised an eyebrow.

"No way," I told her. But something had just happened here, something significant, but something I wasn't in control of. I waved it off.

A few days later, Ken called and asked me to go to lunch. I accepted. We set up a date—though I refused to call it that—working around his daughters' soccer tryouts and my upcoming trip to New York for the James Beard Awards, the awards I had missed the year before to be at my father's side.

We went to lunch at the Columbus Fish Market and were tucked away in a booth at the far side of the dining room. Talking with Ken was easy, but what impressed me the most was his laughter and how easy it came. Here was a man who had lost his wife, his college sweetheart, and was now raising his three young children on his own. But he laughed often and easily, with a joy I couldn't manage on my best days. He didn't brush aside the enormity of what he faced each day, but it didn't seem to drag him down either.

Whatever this man has, I thought as I listened to him laugh and saw the happiness in his eyes, *I want some of that.*

Two months later, I returned to San Francisco to discuss the end of my sabbatical with Michael and Miriam, and I said three words that changed everything: "I've met someone."

It was harder than saying "I love you," words that would come later with Ken and his children. It was an admission that I was changing the course of my life for someone else, something I had never done before. This temporary sabbatical was becoming a permanent resignation.

It was a giant leap of faith, and faith wasn't something I had much faith in. Falling in love wasn't part of the plan, though I had to admit I didn't have much of a plan when I moved to Columbus. But here was a man with whom I was completely comfortable, who didn't care if I was a fancy restaurant critic or a part-time clerk at a gourmet store. Here was someone who understood my grief and whom I could comfort in his. And here was a man who at the end of every date, asked for another one, so I never had to wonder about his feelings for me.

At our wedding two years later, following my sister's toast, while the servers were passing out pieces of our Mad Hatter cake in layers of lemon and chocolate, I offered a toast of my own, paying homage to the circumstances that had made the day possible. The room was filled with my family and Ken's, my friends from San Francisco and Ken's and Grace's from Dayton, and all of Grace's family from her mother and father to her siblings, nieces, and nephews.

"Today," I said, as I looked out, focusing on Grace's family, "I married into not one great family, but two."

This wedding was the epitome of bittersweet. All of us in that room had come so far, but especially Ken, Ben, Molly, Sarah, and I. But we unknowingly had so far to go, miles yet to traverse, hundreds of meals to eat together, thousands of things to learn about each other. Yet at that moment, surrounded by family and friends, old and new, I felt that we had reached the end of the road, not that we were taking the first steps on a new one.

How hard could this be, my new endeavor, I wondered as I looked around the room with my champagne glass raised? I had traveled the world on my own. I had written negative restaurant reviews met with hostile responses. I had cooked dinner parties for dozens and mastered chocolate mousse and soufflés. I was even an accomplished pie maker, turning flour, fat, and water into flakey goodness filled with all kinds of fruits and custards and creams. If I could do all of that, then how hard could it be, really, to be a wife and mother?

Pomegranate Cocktail

Makes 1

I started the tradition of candlelight breakfasts on Valentine's Day the first year we were married. The holiday is, to me, a celebration of love, not just couples. I created this cocktail, with a nonalcoholic version suitable for children, which became the family's celebratory drink on special occasions.

1 tablespoon chilled pomegranate juice

1 cup chilled champagne or sparkling wine

1 teaspoon orange liqueur such as Grand Marnier

Orange peel twist or orange slice for garnish

Pour the pomegranate juice into a champagne flute or wine glass. Fill with champagne.

Top with orange liqueur. Garnish with orange peel or an orange slice.

Serve immediately.

Variation: To make this cocktail nonalcoholic, use nonalcoholic sparkling cider in place of the champagne and orange juice in place of the orange liqueur.

2

The Appetizer

An appetizer is meant to whet the taste buds, get the juices flowing in anticipation of what's to come next. It's a perfect combination of bitter, sweet, and salty flavors with crunchy and silky textures, all in just a bite or two: thin slices of bruschetta topped with jewels of ripe red tomatoes; a single seared scallop wrapped in bacon on a toothpick; a shot glass of vibrant green pea soup with a bit of sour cream and oniony chives on top.

Forming this new relationship—or relationships, really, because it was more than just Ken and me creating a new family—felt exciting, exhilarating. But as often happens with restaurant appetizers that are too big or overly powerful, sometimes it was overwhelming, and it made me wonder if I was ready for the next course. I had no way of knowing that each bite in this new life would be both beautiful and a lot to handle.

I awoke the first morning back from our honeymoon to the sound of a shower running. I sleepily looked over and saw my husband—a new word I would never tire of saying—asleep face down in the bed next to me. If my husband was not the person showering, then who was?

And then I remembered: We were not alone. I was sharing the house not only with the love of my life, but also with his children.

Later I would describe the two years after I left San Francisco as some kind of fairy tale in which I had been sprinkled with pixie dust, plucked out of one situation, and put into another completely different life. My sister put it another way.

"God whispers what he wants most people to do," she said. "But he has to shout at you because you're so stubborn."

It was true. My prayers to God stayed whispers in the beginning, but he made it perfectly clear where he wanted me to be. Yet, I questioned him constantly. Not only did I not have faith in God, but I had little faith in myself.

As Ken and I spent more and more time together that first summer we started dating, he slowly introduced me into the kids' lives. I knew he wanted to move cautiously. Ben, Molly, and Sarah had been through so much; Ken wanted to keep everything in their lives stable and consistent as much as he was able. Ken had made a promise to Grace when she was dying that he and the kids would be fine, and he did everything in his power to make it so.

I wasn't in a giant hurry to move forward with the children anyway. I loved the stories he told me about them. I felt like I knew them. But actually interacting with them? Terrifying.

My experience with children to date had been limited to my almost-year-old nephew. It was a big jump from changing diapers and making silly faces at an infant to conversing with a ten-year-old boy and two eight-year-old girls.

And what if they didn't like me? What if they didn't like their dad dating anyone?

I first met them in passing one day at the house before Ken and I went out to dinner. Ben was still dressed in his black soccer uniform, watching baseball on television. His thick brown hair had a blond patch in front, dyed that color for summer only.

"Ben, this is my friend, Robin," Ken said.

Ben shifted from a lying position to raise himself on an elbow and turned to look at me. "Hi," he mumbled. His enormous blue eyes held mine a few seconds before he turned back to the television.

"Girls!" Ken called. Two sets of footsteps came rumbling down the stairs, and Molly and Sarah blew into the kitchen. They had huge eyes like their brother, and brown hair working its way out of ponytail holders in wispy strands.

"This is Robin," Ken said. The girls looked at me with nothing more than a passing interest, as though I were a new kind of flower they'd never seen.

"This is Molly," Ken said, placing a hand on the head of the slightly taller of the twins, the wavy hair a shade or two lighter than Sarah's.

"And this is Sarah," he said, as she snuggled in next to him with a hug and eyed me curiously.

Ben and Molly looked alike, but Sarah looked just like her dad, save for the eye color that was the same sky blue as her siblings'. The girls were twins but distinctly different in appearance, and as I would later learn, in personalities, too.

And then they were gone, off to the neighbor's house in a flash of hair and flip-flops and brightly colored summer T-shirts, with Ben shuffling behind them.

A few weeks later, Ken suggested dinner at his house, a simple cookout with the kids. I was staggeringly nervous, far more so than

I had ever been on a first date or a job interview. This felt like a terrifying combination of both.

"Just be yourself," Ken reassured me.

Really? I thought. *And who is that?*

I had left a glamorous job in a sophisticated city to move to the
middle of Ohio, where I was now dating a widower with three young
children. Who I was, was a mystery to me these days.

I stuck close to Ken as he made dinner: burgers, salad, fresh fruit.
I watched his interaction with the kids more than I participated.

As Ken put burgers on the grill, Sarah peeked her head out the
screen door and said, "Dad, make sure you make it the way I like it."

"I will, sweetie," he answered.

When she went back inside, I asked Ken what she meant. What
was the secret way Sarah Heigel liked her hamburgers? It seemed an
important thing to know for future reference.

"I have no idea," he said. He continued to make the burgers, all
exactly the same. When we went inside, he put a burger on Sarah's
plate and said, "This one is yours." She loved it.

Later in the same meal, as we were gathered around the circular
dinner table, Molly said, "Dad, can we make the table big again?"

After Grace died, Ken had taken the leaf from the table, turning
it from an oval into a round and hoping that, by making it smaller,
they wouldn't have to be reminded of their loss every single night at
dinner.

Ken glanced at me, then at Molly and said, "Maybe we can."

After that first meal together, Ken started integrating the kids more
into our dates. We went apple picking one Sunday afternoon, and I
taught them to make an apple pie. Two things I learned: Kids' hands

aren't big enough for adult tools such as vegetable peelers, and kids have a limited interest in the same activity for a long period of time. They each peeled a single apple, but that was about it. I finished putting the pie together myself.

But they were impressed with the size of the pie—I used every apple we picked—and we enjoyed it at the end of the day.

Food would become a language all of us could understand. I didn't know squat about motherhood or soccer or whatever eight-year-old twins might be thinking, but there wasn't too much they could ask me about food or cooking that I couldn't answer or even demonstrate.

One day, I took Sarah grocery shopping with me, and she asked me rapid-fire questions about produce.

"What's this?" she asked, holding up a head of ordinary green cabbage.

"That's cabbage." I pointed to red, napa, and savoy varieties. "And that and that and that are cabbage, too."

"What's that?" She pointed to a rutabaga.

"That's a rutabaga. It's kind of like this turnip but with a little bit of a tan."

Sarah smiled.

"OK, what's this?" she asked, holding up a drippy bunch of Swiss chard with stems the size of her skinny forearm.

"It's Swiss chard. And that right next to it? It's rainbow chard. See the different colors of the stems?"

We went that way all around the produce section. When we got home, she ran into the house. "Dad! Dad! Robin knows everything at the grocery store!"

That autumn, Ken invited me to Dayton for Ben's soccer tournament and to meet his family. When we piled into the family van that Friday afternoon, the kids seemed to pick up that this was some big milestone, though Ken and I had continued to maintain to them that we were just friends. Nonetheless they seemed quiet and nervous in the backseat. Soon they started singing a song they had learned that day at school. Over and over they sang the little song, "dip-dip and swing" in sweet young voices, as though the sound soothed them.

We spent the weekend at the home of Ken's sister Karen. His mother and father, his other sister Kim, and all the cousins came around at different times to meet me. Ben, Molly, and Sarah spent most of their free time with Katie and Kevin, Karen's kids.

When we were driving back home Sunday afternoon, we decided spur of the moment to stop at an outlet mall and go into the Disney store. Ken and I were walking through the store talking to one another, unaware that the kids were huddled together and whispering.

Sarah walked up to me, putting on a bold face, and said, "Robin, are you married?"

"I'm not," I answered.

Sarah covered her mouth, giggled, and ran back to the other two. More whispering ensued.

She ran back up to me. "Do you have any kids?"

"I do not."

Sarah squealed and ran back to Molly and Ben.

Ken and I looked at each other with raised eyebrows. The older cousins seemed to have filled in the kids on what their dad's "friend" might really be. And if this reaction was any indication, they were excited by the possibilities.

In February, I closed on a condo not far from Ken and the kids, upgrading from the apartment I had moved into a year before. The first night I owned the place, the five of us ordered pizza and spent the evening painting. I had chosen a sage green for most of the living space and a warm pleasant yellow for my bedroom.

Ken and Ben set to painting the living room. Molly, Sarah, and I painted my bedroom.

Ken had instructed the kids to be careful with the paint, always work with a tarp, and not get too much paint on the roller. The kids knew to take the job seriously.

In the bedroom, I was working on cutting the edges near the ceiling with a brush while the girls took to rolling the walls down below. I looked down and noticed that Molly had stopped. She had rolled a portion of her brush over the cover on the electrical outlet and was just staring at the yellow paint on the beige plastic cover. She had not been careful.

I came down from the ladder, picked up a rag, and wiped off the paint. I looked at her and shrugged. "It's pretty easy to clean up a little mess," I said.

She beamed at me.

We heard the boys laughing in the living room, so we went to investigate. They had started applying paint to the wall that I wanted to be the accent wall, a bold dark brown called "truffle."

Ken and Ben were lying on the floor, laughing at the big area they had painted.

"It looks like a black hole!" Ken laughed.

"It looks like baby poop!" said Ben.

We all giggled and decided that despite its enticing name, the color was indeed too dark. I'd never be able to look at it without thinking of baby poop.

"Where's Sarah?" Molly asked, ever mindful of where her twin was.

Just then, Sarah came out from a closet off the hallway, carrying a little can of paint and a paintbrush.

"All done," she said proudly.

Ken and I went to look. On the back wall of the closet of my new home she had painted, S M B K R—our initials, altogether in a row.

I reached over and hugged her, kissing the top of her head.

As I began to integrate into the family, my whisper prayers started to sound more like an actual dialogue. It went something like this:

"What if you and Ken got married?" God would ask.

"But I don't want to get married."

"You could be a stepmother to Ben, Molly, and Sarah."

"I would be a terrible mother."

"I think you can do it."

That's usually where the dialogue stopped, my internal voice silenced with fear.

Where was this coming from, this deep feeling of being called to be a wife and mother, two things I was certain I neither wanted to be, nor would be good at? I didn't usually struggle with myself. I decided what I wanted—and what I didn't want—and lived by those decisions. But here I was with an internal conflict, wanting something I wasn't sure I wanted at all, at the same time, in the same breath.

When I look back now, I know the struggle wasn't really with me or within myself. It was with what I felt God was calling me to do, which happened to be one thing I had told myself for years that I didn't want.

But there was no denying that the children really did like me, which on its own was a sign of God's grace. They could have been resentful, distrustful, and hurt that their father would fall in love with someone other than their mother. But they were none of those things.

They were beautiful children with beautiful hearts that, despite the death of their mother, were full and open and loving. They had no doubts in me—which was good, because I had so many of my own. What could I offer them? What kind of a stepmother would I be?

I'd always seen motherhood as a losing proposition. Few women get it just right. And stepmotherhood? No one wins at that. You're constantly compared to the biological mother. And when she happened to be a mother who died so young and tragically and bravely, it's a losing hand before the cards are even dealt.

Months passed, and I fell more in love with Ken and the children every day, to a point that I simply couldn't imagine my life without them. But always the internal reservations bubbled just below the surface. I felt in the deepest part of my soul God's presence: his watching, his nodding and nudging, asking me to trust him, to believe in where he had brought me.

In December, in a dark theater at a holiday pops concert of the Columbus Symphony Chorus, Ken took my hand and slipped a ring on my finger. "Will you marry me?" he whispered.

That moment felt like the actual calling from God, as though he were saying, "I want you to marry this man. I want you to be a mother to these children." It couldn't have been any clearer if the angel Gabriel had come and told me himself that this was God's plan for me. Did I have the courage to say yes to Ken, to say yes to God?

I closed my eyes, took a deep breath, and with my heart pounding, said, "Yes. I'll marry you."

And so here I was waking up in a new house, with a husband and three children, one of them showering down the hall. My nerves jangled with anxiety.

Ken felt me sit up and stirred, turning over to look at me. He smiled. "Good morning, wife," he said.

I slunk back down under the covers with him, instantly soothed. "Who's in the shower?" I asked him.

"Probably Ben, getting ready for Mass."

It was Sunday, and the kids knew we'd be going to Mass. It wasn't a discussion.

At Mass that Sunday, many well-wishers who had either been to or heard about our wedding the week before greeted us. I felt like I was on display, wearing a mask, like you feel on the first day of a new job, hoping you'll come across as competent and won't do something stupid you'll always be remembered for.

I didn't do anything stupid, necessarily, but it was anything but an easy transition. I felt out of place, like I didn't fit in, and unable to decide what exactly I was supposed to be doing. I kept thinking, *This is the first day of the rest of your life.* But I didn't have an instruction book, a guide telling me precisely what I was supposed to do.

Even everyday activities felt stilted. When I went to make coffee, the kids jumped at the sound of the coffee grinder. When they moved to get breakfast, we bumped into one another in the kitchen.

After Mass, sensing my anxiety, Ken suggested we open wedding presents, with so many boxes having been delivered while we were on our honeymoon. The kids sat with us and watched, but with an anxious air about them, too, as though they were at a family event they couldn't wait to be done with.

Finally, I did the one thing that came naturally to me: I went to the kitchen.

I took stock of what was in the cupboards and the refrigerator. I asked the kids what they liked to eat for breakfast, and I planned a week of meals. With a list in hand, I headed to the grocery store.

My sanctuary had always been the kitchen, where I went when I was sad, when I was happy, and when I didn't know where else to go.

When I speak at public events or teach a cooking class, people often ask me how long food has been my passion. I always respond, "I've been eating my whole life."

I originally found comfort in the kitchen because that is where I usually found my mother. With three older brothers, one-on-one time with her was scarce. The boys didn't care about cooking, so if I wanted time with Mom without them, it pretty much had to be in the kitchen.

My mother was an excellent cook. She had grown up on a farm in Southern Illinois and learned to cook at her own mother's side. She subscribed to *Gourmet* magazine, but her own cooking was pure home-style: pot roast, chicken-fried steak, fried chicken, meat loaf.

Other family favorites took on the flavors of where we went or people we knew. My father was in the Air Force, and when I was three, we moved to Germany. From there came sauerbraten and warm German-style potato salad usually served with grilled bratwurst.

My parents became friends with a Chinese couple through Dad's work, and a few times a year, the two wives would have an egg-roll making day. They would make so many we could pack them into the freezer and heat them up one by one in the microwave when one of us missed family dinner because of sports or cheerleading or choir practice.

But despite my mother's apparent love of cooking, she also had a great love of convenience products that had been a novelty to her when she was growing up. I didn't have a made-from-scratch cake until I moved to California, nor did I have long-simmered pasta sauce because the staple on our table was Ragu.

It was a dichotomy I would ponder later, but as a child, I loved being with Mom in the kitchen whether we were making her legendary smothered steak in onion gravy from scratch or rolling crescent rolls from a can.

It's not really surprising, then, that when Mom died, my family assumed that I would take on her role. Cooking equals motherhood. The problem was, in my book, it didn't.

My mother's death was a surprise. She didn't die suddenly in some kind of accident, but I was as ill prepared for it as if she had. The whole situation was off script, not only because a mother isn't supposed to die when the child is just twenty-two, but also because she died of alcoholism. I didn't know someone could die from alcoholism—not just acute alcohol poisoning but from the rupturing of the esophagus, tearing of the lining of the heart, and of course, from horrible cirrhosis of the liver.

Halfway through my senior year at UD, my mother was rushed to the hospital with intense stomach pains and coughs that left her spitting up blood. My sixteen-year-old sister called to tell me that Mom was an alcoholic.

But that was all wrong. Dad, *Dad* was the heavy drinker. Mom just had her one drink in the evening.

"You mean the never-empty scotch and soda?" my brother, Mark, asked when we gathered at Christmas, with Mom still in the hospital but scheduled for release in a few days.

It was true. It was a magic drink, one that never emptied, one in which the ice never melted, but one that we never saw her refill.

"Or the bloody Mary at lunch?" Dorothy said.

"Or the 'cough syrup' in the morning?" Scott said, telling us that this was Mom's code for Jäegermeister. She would have a shot or two of that every morning when she got up. Then the bloody Mary or two at lunch. A gin and tonic with Dad when he got home from work—a ritual I had always viewed as somehow glamorous. And finally, the magic scotch-and-soda.

Each of us had a piece to the puzzle of Mom's disease, but each piece, on its own, hadn't looked that bad. Our mother wasn't a falling-down drunk. In fact, I don't know that I ever saw her *drunk*. Or maybe I never actually saw her sober. Looking back, it's hard to tell.

After she died, of course, we looked at all the signs and wondered how we had missed them. We were blind to her condition, but we wondered if Dad was, too. Had he known the severity of her drinking problem? Or had he been too afraid to address it because that would have forced him to confront his own drinking habits?

The day my mother died, just a week after my college graduation, my father called from the hospital to tell me she was gone. Before I had a chance to grieve, he appointed me the stand-in matriarch, asking me to get my sister home from school and call all the other relatives, including my grandfather, my mother's father. I wrote the obituary and planned her funeral service and the wake.

Later, my family turned to me to plan the holidays, which I tried to do, but with little enthusiasm. The first Thanksgiving after Mom's death, we ate at the restaurant at a nearby Holiday Inn because I wasn't yet ready to tackle cooking an entire Thanksgiving dinner. That dinner was dreadful, made even more unbearable by the happy families—complete families—around us.

Christmas was the same, a time that reminded us of loss more than a time of newborn happiness and promise for the new year. I resented the role of being the "mother," because I was as lost and confused as everyone else.

When my head cleared enough for me to gather my thoughts, I finally told myself, *Enough. Enough of this madness of trying to be something I am not.*

I started cleaning up what my life had become by ending the bad romantic relationship with the much older man I had maintained since college. And not surprisingly, it ended as badly as it had continued, with shouts and threats and broken windows. But once the dust settled, I had a newfound strength, and another reason to look around my life and see what else had to go.

How about this city? I thought. *How about I say good-bye to Dayton, too?*

I requested, and was granted, a transfer at the computer company where I had worked in marketing since graduation. I packed what little I had, leaving the detritus of my life behind, and moved to San Diego.

I left not only my family, but God as well. Maybe I hadn't been perfect, but I had been faith-filled, I thought. Why hadn't God intervened? Why hadn't he saved my mother? Why couldn't he show my family some way to carry on without her? Somewhere along the way, I had come to believe that bad things didn't happen to people of faith—though there was plenty of evidence to the contrary in the world around me.

"If this is what you have to offer," I told God, with my know-it-all, twenty-three-year-old attitude, "I'm not interested."

From now on, I was in charge. No God. No needy boyfriend. No clingy family.

And for the next ten years or so, it worked pretty well. I fought hard for a new career in food, something I truly loved: the creation, the nourishment it brought people, and also the joy. I sent myself to the California Culinary Academy in San Francisco, then spent years studying and writing about my newfound devotion.

Food and cooking became my passion, my obsession: my religion. The two aren't that actually far apart. There's a theory that if someone who knows nothing about Christianity reads the Bible for the first time, he'll go away believing that it's about food—from the dietary restrictions and the manna from heaven of the Old Testament to the New Testament's loaves and fishes, the wedding at Cana, and finally, the breaking of the bread, the Eucharist. During my years in California, I walked a kind of parallel life with religion, though I didn't know it at the time.

I studied at the table of the earth, learning how foods were grown and raised, how farmers and ranchers worked with weather and land to create ingredients that could be made into meals. I learned at the hands of chefs and home cooks, who took these ingredients and prepared them to feed and to nourish, whether for customers to make a living or for families to make a life. What could have been more basic and holy than that?

I may have abolished organized religion and church from my life, but I worshipped what God gave us, even if I didn't give him credit at the time. I was fascinated the first time I tasted a fresh fig with its spongy insides behind a leathery skin, and diligent when a Jewish mother taught me how to braid yeasted dough into challah and how to caramelize onions slowly to grind into chopped liver. I sought to discern the nuances of a pinot noir made from grapes grown in Sonoma versus one produced in the Burgundy region of France.

I ate off the plates of some of the country's best chefs, savoring sea urchin from a sushi chef in Los Angeles, truffle risotto at a fine dining restaurant in San Francisco, and broccoli rabe dressed with the gooey golden yolk of a barely cooked duck egg at a downscale Italian hot spot in New York. I broke bread in boulangeries from San Francisco to Paris, always finding time to crack open a baguette or enjoy one more crusty slice turned faintly purple from walnuts or studded bitter with salty black olives.

I took these lessons and applied them in my own kitchens, both at home and at work. It was pure joy to spend an evening rendering fat from the skin of a duck and later using it to sauté thin slices of potatoes or shredded leaves of chard. I continued to tamper with a recipe for Brussels sprouts, pasta, and egg just hours before I was to catch a flight to London, when I knew I wouldn't be in a kitchen for days.

Food and cooking were my daily prayers, my constant meditations, the underlying lifeblood of my very existence.

Now, here I was, far away from the life I had so carefully crafted, and well into a life that God—the same God I had purposefully and methodically walked away from—had called me to.

While it had seemed so clear that he had wanted me to marry Ken and be a mother to Ben, Molly, and Sarah, it was less apparent to me what exactly he wanted me to do now that I was here. So I set up my temple in the kitchen of our new family home and continued the only prayers I knew: the stirring, bubbling, melding prayers of cooking, while I waited for further divine instructions.

Prosciutto-Wrapped Asparagus

Makes about 20

We served this appetizer at our wedding, but it also is a go-to dish for dinner parties. Sometimes I go the extra step of wrapping the asparagus and prosciutto in phyllo dough, but usually I find the process too time-consuming and fussy. The combination of asparagus and the salty Italian ham are a family favorite. We enjoy it on everything from pizza to pasta. Don't use pencil-thin asparagus spears, but thicker ones. If they're too thin, they'll burn before the prosciutto gets crispy.

1 tablespoon olive oil

1 bunch fresh asparagus spears (about 20), trimmed

Kosher salt

Freshly ground black pepper

10 paper-thin slices prosciutto, halved lengthwise

½ cup freshly grated Parmesan cheese

Preheat oven to 450 degrees. Line a baking sheet with foil.

Drizzle asparagus with oil, tossing to coat. Season lightly with salt and pepper. Wrap one prosciutto slice around each spear, leaving tip end exposed. Arrange on baking sheet.

Roast 5 minutes. Turn spears over. Roast until asparagus is tender and prosciutto is crisp, about 5 minutes longer. Sprinkle with Parmesan cheese. Serve warm or at room temperature.

3

The Soup

The thing about soup is, it can be thick and chunky or smooth and creamy—and just about every variation in between.

Smooth purees take the most work, I think. The ingredients need to be roasted or sautéed or simmered until soft, but in a way that retains or intensifies their flavors. And smooth soups tend to require fewer ingredients, so each one has to be top quality for the best results.

Like a silky puree, early family life for us was mostly smooth sailing, though it wasn't necessarily carefree. We all worked hard in those early months and years to make the best of what we had been given.

Food was, I believed, the only thing I could really give the children. I didn't have natural motherhood instincts or intuition. I wasn't wildly playful or adventurous like some kind of super babysitter. But I could make them just about any food they wanted, so I made dinner almost every night, plus breakfast on weekends and packed lunches during the week. As long as I made it with love, I hoped it would be enough.

But cooking for my new family did present a few challenges.

When Grace was sick, planning meals had fallen dramatically on the priority chart. When her illness grew serious, neighbors set up a schedule to bring food to the family. The refrigerator and freezer became stocked with casseroles and other dishes that lent themselves to being reheated. The family became reliant on, and grateful for, the tastes and skills of others to feed them.

After Grace died, Ken did what he could to lighten the burden of caring for a family entirely on his own. One step was hiring a personal chef. Once a week she would come to the house and cook, leaving that evening's meal for the family and stocking the refrigerator and freezer with other dishes that reheated well.

When I entered the scene, neither Ken nor the kids could tell me much about what they liked to eat. They had stuck pretty much to the basics: tacos, grilled cheese sandwiches, plain buttered pasta. There were few family favorites. That left me something of a blank slate, which should have been great. However, since I was dealing with children, I quickly learned that I had to tread slowly. Ken might love my seared day-boat scallops with a fresh corn relish, but it wasn't going to fly with Ben, Molly, and Sarah.

The first thing I needed to realize was that I couldn't take food personally when it came to the kids. After a few missteps, I treated family meals like something of a puzzle, trying new things here and there to see what would fit. If they liked pasta baked with tomato sauce and they liked hamburgers, would they like spaghetti and meatballs and lasagna? The answer was yes to both. Quesadillas and macaroni and cheese were favorites, so it should follow that cheese enchiladas would work. For reasons I still don't quite understand, that was a no. When they didn't like something, they would tell me,

"It's not my favorite." And Ben would then sweetly follow up with, "But I really like the milk tonight!"

I also wanted to use the dinner table to teach nutrition to some degree. We almost always had a fruit and a vegetable at dinner, and I slowly moved the family from instant rice to long-grain white rice, then brown rice, and from white pasta to multigrain.

Many of their preferences had to do with their ages. I've read studies showing that children may not accept new foods until they've tried them as many as fifteen times. I had to patiently continue to serve them nutritious and delicious foods without making the dinner table a battleground. When I was offering something new at dinner, I made sure there was something else on the table that they already liked, so no one would go hungry. And we had a standing policy that if someone really didn't like what was for dinner, they could have yogurt or cereal instead.

No one ever did. Not once.

One of the greatest things I learned from my family is that they were big fans of my food. Years in the food business had turned me into my own harshest critic. I would fume if I cooked a pizza crust a little too dark or if a pork chop or chicken breast was a smidge dry.

But to my family, dinner was always about more than food. The dinner table was our guaranteed time and place for gathering together. Ken and I took turns getting the kids off to school, and we alternated who was picking up whom and when and from where. But several times a week, we sat together at the table in our kitchen and shared a meal.

Every meal started by saying grace. "Bless us, O Lord, for these thy gifts which we are about to receive from thy bounty through Christ our Lord." It was a brief moment when, no matter what I was feeling and no matter what kind of day I'd had, no matter what my fears and doubts might be, I could just thank God for the gift of this food, a gift small but great.

After grace, we played a game we called "high/low." Each family member would tell the best part of his or her day, then the worst. We almost always had more highs than lows.

One night, I asked Ken where the game had come from. He smiled. "When we were first married, Grace hated her job, working third shift at an envelope factory. She would complain and complain about it. So I started asking her at the end of every day, 'Tell me five things that were good today, and five things that were bad.'"

"So it was a game you played with the children when Grace was still alive?"

"No. They were really too young, then," he said. "I started playing it with the kids after she died."

I could picture it clearly: all of them sitting around the table, now round instead of oval with the leaf removed and the fifth chair taken away. I could feel Ken's pain, so palpable at the loss. I could hear him saying to himself, *Where's the positive?* And I could hear him echoing to the children what he'd said to his wife, "What's the best thing and the worst thing that happened today? What's your high and your low?"

And in hearing the things the kids had loved that day—a chocolate-covered peanut butter bar at lunch, an extra fifteen minutes of recess, an A on a test—he had been able to find good in his heartbroken world.

Family meals also gave us a bridge to cross into a safe zone, away from school and work, where just the five of us could be together. Food was a great conversation starter. Almost before they said "hello"

the kids would ask what was for dinner. Not in a demanding way, but an excited, "I-can't-wait" way. And if I was feeling awkward or not quite connected to them, the question always opened a door for me. If I'm comfortable talking about one thing, it's food.

"Tonight we're having homemade tomato soup with cheese toasts!"

I might get a dubious look. I might get a "Have we had that before?" But the ice was broken, and I could then tell them more about it and why I thought they might like it.

This was particularly handy when the kids went from preteen to teen. Their moods were more erratic, and sullenness sometimes set in. Ben, Molly, and Sarah were probably better than most teenagers, but often I felt that conversing with them was about as effective as shouting instructions for surgery through a megaphone to a person on a desert island I could barely see from shore.

Food has a remarkable way of being a rowboat between two seemingly distance places, though. The aromas of lemon juice hitting a hot pan of sautéing chicken, or beef stew bubbling away in a slow cooker would coax them out of their teenage angst. Almost against their will, they would still ask, "What's for dinner?" And the conversation door swung open.

It was at the dinner table that I first started to see my influence on the kids, as they became mirrors of me. I saw myself, heard myself, first through Molly.

Ken told me that when the girls were babies, he usually held Sarah, and Grace held Molly. He didn't remember how it started or why, but by the time the girls were toddlers, they had chosen their respective parents. If Ken picked up Molly, she would wiggle and squirm until he handed her to Grace. And vice-versa with Sarah. The attachments led on into childhood, partly because Ken and Sarah were so much alike in their appearances and their bubbly personalities. So when Grace died, seven-year-old Molly was, in some ways, on her own. She and Sarah were close, in a way only twins can be, but she didn't have that favorite parent anymore, as Sarah did.

By the time I met Molly, I sensed her strong spirit and independence. She is quieter than Sarah, and even at a young age, was more cerebral. She preferred independent study to group projects and was just as happy reading a book as playing games with the rest of us.

At the beginning I was the most hesitant with Molly. Ben and I were close almost from the start. I could fill that outside void with him that made him seem different to other kids. And I could talk sports and make cookies. What was there for a young boy not to like? In Sarah's case, as long as I made her dad happy—and never stood in the way of their closeness—we'd get along just fine. But what to make of Molly?

I remember being at one of Ken's family gatherings early in our relationship, watching the interactions a little from a distance, as I'm likely to do. Before long, Molly was standing right in front of me, facing the same way, almost leaning into me, also watching. I wanted so badly to just wrap my arms around her, but I wasn't sure if that would cross some kind of invisible barrier. I did nothing.

At another event a few weeks later, Molly and I were both sitting on an ottoman, face to face, our heads leaning over a magazine, forming a tent of hair, hardly speaking, just flipping the pages.

"Look at that," I heard Ken's sister, Karen, whisper to him. "They look so much alike."

I thought, *You are seeing what you want to see.* Molly and I look nothing alike. She is willowy and angular and has an oval face, compared to my short curvy roundness. And as she's gotten older, the differences, especially in height, have only grown more dramatic.

The truth is, Molly and I have the same temperament. We're less likely to be the most outspoken person in a group. We like small group interaction or, better yet, one-on-one time with family and friends. We're not fond of drama; we find it a waste of time and energy. And we like our alone time, when we can gather our thoughts, renew our spirits, and do what we want without outside influence.

It was with Molly that I first heard myself, as parents do with their children: words and phrases, and a tone that on occasion, sounded as if it came out of my own mouth. So it was with Molly that I had to learn to temper what I might say and how I would say it, especially when it came to her father.

Ken and I jest a lot together. Making the other laugh is one of the great joys of our marriage. He is the engineer, so he playfully likes to say he knows everything. I'm well read and a news junky, so I like to spar with him, especially on current events, spewing facts that stick in my head. By the end of a battle, he usually covers his head in his hands, and laughs, acknowledging that the volume of information I can throw at him overwhelms his scientific reasoning.

One night at dinner, we were beginning to spar. Ben and Sarah were giggling, then Molly said with disdain, "Dad, what facts do you have to support that?"

I knew the tone the instant I heard it. It was mine. I use an exaggerated version of it when I want to make a point, and with Ken, it was part of our shtick. Hearing it coming back at me, however, I realized how it might sound to a ten-year-old: Like I thought her dad was an idiot. Clearly, I needed to dial back that tone. But more important, that same night I realized that, in a sense, I had become Molly's chosen parent. I would need to tread carefully with that responsibility. It wasn't hard to do because when it came to the kids, "careful" was my middle name.

Except when it came to food fights, for which I had a penchant. Every so often, I would get the urge to fill my mouth with grapes and spit them across the table at Ken, much to the kids' delight. Occasionally, while Ken and the kids were talking during dinner, I would balance a cherry tomato on a fork, then, when there was a break in the conversation, I would launch it at an unsuspecting victim.

That was about as close to Mary Poppins or Maria Von Trapp that I got. Most of the time, I was more reserved, wary of giving the children the wrong image of me.

One gift I received from being a stepmother was the impetus to become a better cook. In my professional life, I had developed recipes for years—for stories, books, and consulting. But all of that was a means to an end. Cooking is completely different when you do it for people you know and love. I like my readers, but giving them a printed recipe that I've tested isn't the same as putting a plate of food in front of people and watching them eat it.

Much of my improved techniques came simply from practice. I had all the skills necessary to cook, but I used them sporadically before marriage and stepmotherhood. The more nights I spent cooking, the better I got at it.

I didn't just make everyday dinner; I started taking on holiday meals for the extended family, too. Columbus is in the middle of Ohio, which put us right between Ken's brother who lived in Cleveland up north and his sisters and parents, who lived in Dayton, about an hour west. When we were deciding where to have Thanksgiving after we were married, our house was the best choice. Everyone could drive there and back in the same day.

Ken and his siblings worried that it was too much work for me, but cooking was actually my salvation. In my kitchen, I always had something to do. I didn't have to worry about awkward silences or figuring out how to react to stories from before I joined the family. I could baste the turkey or mash potatoes or whisk the gravy; I was better at those things than at conversation anyway.

And I would be in charge of the food, which, to be honest, is how I like things.

I tell my readers at the newspaper that Thanksgiving is actually one of the easiest meals to cook. After you've cooked it once or twice, you get the hang of it, you feel the rhythm of the dinner. Little, if anything, changes on the menu. At my work for the newspaper food section, I usually end up making one or two Thanksgiving dinners of some sort for stories I'm writing. By the time the holiday rolls around, my skills are honed. This is a good thing, because, when we gather all the family from my side, Ken's side, and Grace's side, we often host twenty-five to thirty people.

Ken and I work beautifully together when we're hosting a party. I handle the kitchen, and he handles cleaning the house, setting the table, and washing the dishes (although the guests usually help a lot with the cleanup).

Not much makes me as happy as watching people pile the food on their plates and come back for seconds, gathering around the dining room table and kitchen table, or crowding onto the couches. I like to say that our house is happiest when it's full of people because I believe I can feel God in all the laughter. God has called us all to live in community, and holiday meals with all the families blended together represents that perfectly to me.

Thanksgiving worked so well, we started hosting Christmas, too. And then occasional other gatherings. St. Patrick's Day feasts, however, naturally fell to Grace's mother, Pat, because she and Jim were both first-generation Irish-American. Our gatherings those days weren't big, usually just the five of us and the two of them. And like Thanksgiving, the menu didn't change: corned beef and cabbage,

boiled red-skin potatoes, soda bread studded with raisins and car-
away seeds.

When Ben was in eighth grade, the holiday fell at the same time
as the school musical. Molly and Sarah were both in it, and Ben
had the lead, playing Harold Hill in the *Music Man*. Ken's parents
and some friends of Pat's were scheduled to join us for a meal before
the big show. But in the weeks prior to the musical, Pat had a heart
attack. The damage was minimal and the blockage easily fixed with
a stent, but she was in no condition to cook for a houseful.

"I'll do it," I told Ken.

I didn't have enough vacation time to take off the holiday, which
fell on a Thursday. Instead, I researched cooking corned beef in a
slow cooker, adding wedges of cabbage to the pot when I got home
to steam them just slightly. I boiled potatoes and tossed them with
plenty of butter, and turned soda bread into muffins, which were
easier for me to manage and took less time to bake. A traditional
Irish meal was on the table in plenty of time for us to make it to
Music Man.

Later that night after the kids were in bed, Ken and I plopped
ourselves down on the couch, just leaning into each other.

"Do you know what my mom said about you tonight?" he asked.

I turned to look at him. "What?"

"She said you work so hard," Ken said, taking my hands in his and
rubbing them. "And you do. You work so hard to make everything
just right for everyone."

Some things, like Mother's Day, remained complicated. Before I was
married, I had spent years hiding on Mother's Day, so I didn't have
to see happy families and people celebrating their moms when I

didn't have one any longer. I had never mastered or even really tried to simply honor my mother's memory and be grateful for the time I'd had with her.

Now I was living with three kids who had also lost their mother.

The first Mother's Day after Grace died was just weeks after Ken and I met again. He told me that the kids had made Mother's Day cards for him that year, while the rest of the classmates made cards for their moms. It was a sweet and heartfelt gesture, but a prelude to the discomfort the day would bring in years to come.

The kids' teachers, knowing of their loss, tried to make the holiday manageable for them, but their efforts were not especially successful. The next year, Sarah's teacher asked her if she'd like to file for her while the rest of the class made cards. Molly was given the option of reading, which of course she did, losing herself in a book instead of dealing with potential sadness. Ben chose to write a letter to his dad as he had the year before. But in the end, all these well-meaning activities just made the children feel different and excluded, making their loss all the more apparent to them.

In the years that followed, the children had a stepmother, so whatever their classes did for the moms, they were just expected to do for me. The problem was, it made me wildly uncomfortable. I didn't want them to feel obligated to do anything for me. If they felt the desire to do something, make a card, or buy a gift, that was fine. But I couldn't bear for them to feel forced when possibly the holiday made them miss their mom, as I did mine.

The first year after we married, we went to Mass on Mother's Day. At the end of the service, the priest asked all mothers to kneel and for their children to place their hands on them while he gave a special blessing. I didn't kneel. I just honestly didn't believe it applied to me.

Ken stared at me. The kids looked at him, then at me and back to him. Finally he put his hand on my shoulder and gently pushed down. I kneeled and was blessed, but felt like a fake.

"I'm not a mom," I told him later when we were alone.

"You *are* a mom," he said. "You are Ben, Molly, and Sarah's mom on earth."

"I'm a *step*mom," I said. "Not a biological mom."

"I don't think the priest said for all biological moms to kneel. He said all moms. You are a mom."

It was a discussion we would have many times, and in many forms, through the years.

I walked a fine line in this new realm of motherhood. I was their stepmother, a title with no real legal standing, but also the only mother they would now have on earth. And what I was, who I was, sometimes became muddled by social customs and expectations.

The day before our wedding, I took Molly and Sarah to have their nails done. They would be wearing ivory dresses, so I gave them the choice of a bright red or pearly pink for their fingers and toes, the same colors I would be wearing.

We each ended up in different areas of the spa, so I wasn't with them while they were having their nails done. When we were in the car on the way home, Sarah said, "The lady who did my nails said my mom chose the color for me."

I glanced in the rearview mirror at her. She looked troubled. She caught my eyes. "I didn't know what to say," she murmured.

"Sarah, we're always going to have people who assume certain things about us," I told her. "You have to ask yourself if it's important to clarify it or not. If it's a friend or someone's mom, you can just say, 'She's my stepmom.' But people like today? You don't have to explain it to her. . . . Unless it's important to you," I added quickly.

She looked relieved, and smiled.

I struggled also with my name and how to be identified outside our immediate family. Should I take Ken's name after we were married? I wrote professionally under my maiden name, so I thought I should keep it for work. But what about more personal situations?

I asked Ken. "It really doesn't matter to me," he said. And I knew it didn't. "But you know people will still call you Robin Heigel, don't you?" he asked. That didn't matter to me.

The day of my confirmation at our church retreat before the Easter vigil service, I prayed about whether or not to change my name. Would our family seem more unified if we all had the same name? Was keeping my own name a way of not committing completely to the marriage?

At the end of the retreat, Deacon Frank Iannarino, who ran the adult Catholic initiation program at St. Brigid, told us a story about how he got his name. Usually in the Italian tradition, the first boy child is to be named after the father. But Frank had an uncle, one he had never known, who died. His grandfather decided that this new child would be named Francis after this uncle, instead of after him and his own first-born son.

"Your parents are your first teachers of the faith," Frank told us, "Whether you agree with what they taught or didn't teach, out of respect for your parents, you should keep that name."

I took it to heart literally, and I kept my last name.

Often when the kids were in school, teachers and other parents called me Mrs. Heigel. It never bothered me, and I rarely felt the need to correct anyone about it. It did, however, create stumbling blocks for some of the kids' friends, especially in high school, when the kids and their friends were at an age you could have real conversations with them.

"Hi, Mr. Heigel," they'd say when they saw Ken or he answered the door to our house.

I would get, "Hi . . .," followed by an awkward pause that I would often fill in with, "Robin. Just call me Robin."

Some did, but not many. It broke some kind of taboo they weren't ready to deal with in high school. But it never fazed me. With a rare sense of self-clarity in this new role, I knew who I was, and I didn't need a name or a title.

Sometimes, however, I did use the "step" in parent as a barrier, often followed in my head by the words *not real*. If someone complimented me on the children, I was quick to brush it off, giving credit to Ken and thinking, *I'm not their real mother.*

For reasons I don't quite understand, I even tried at one point to explain it all to my nephew, Josh, when he was about five. I was at my sister's house, and Josh had settled next to me on the couch. We were talking about families, something particularly interesting to him because he now had a new brother.

"You know how Freddie is your brother?" I asked him.

He nodded.

"Your mom is my sister."

His eyes got wide. What a concept: His mom could be a mom *and* a sister.

"And you're Ben, Molly, and Sarah's mom," Josh said, putting the equation together in the other direction; I could be a mom and a sister, too.

"Well, not exactly," I said. He looked at me, a tiny furrow between his eyes.

"Remember how Freddie was in your mom's tummy?" I asked him.

He nodded.

"Ben, Molly and Sarah were never in my tummy."

"Why not?"

"They had another mommy."

Josh looked at me, clearly disbelieving. He knew, even at five, that sometimes adults liked to simplify things for little kids. He was interested in the whole story, and if he didn't get it, he would fill in whatever blanks we might leave with wild stories that could only come from a child's mind.

"No, you're Ben, Molly, and Sarah's mommy," he said.

"I'm their *step*-mommy." I emphasized the word "step" as I often did so as to not take any responsibility or credit for anything they might do.

"What's that?" he asked.

"Well, I married Uncle Ken after Ben, Molly, and Sarah were born. So I'm not their real mom. I'm called their stepmom."

Again, the look of disbelief.

My sister's husband, Rich, had come downstairs and was listening to the conversation play out. "Josh," he said, smiling, "the only steps in this family are the ones that go up stairs."

I looked at Josh and saw the resolution pass over his little face. Clearly, he was willing to take his dad's explanation at face value.

And in the end, that was the explanation that was closest to the truth anyway. *Step* is just a prefix. And when you're the only mom in the home, day to day, *step* doesn't mean very much.

Tomato and Roasted Garlic Soup with Cheese Toasts

Makes 4 to 6 servings

There are many nights when we eat the standard canned cream of tomato soup and grilled cheese sandwiches. But when I have a little extra time, I make this version. You can make the roasted garlic a day or two ahead. And why not roast some extra heads while you're at it? The meltingly soft cloves are delicious pureed with a little olive oil, then spread on toasted baguette slices.

3 medium heads garlic

4 tablespoons olive oil

1 large onion, chopped

1 tablespoon chopped fresh rosemary or 1 teaspoon crushed dried

**1 tablespoon chopped fresh thyme or
1 teaspoon dried**

Pinch of sugar

Kosher salt to taste

3 cans (14½ ounces each) diced tomatoes with juices

3 cups canned low-salt vegetable broth

1 bay leaf

1 baguette, cut into ½-inch-thick slices

½ cup grated asiago, Parmesan, or Romano cheese

Preheat oven to 375 degrees.

Cut the top ¼-inch off the heads of garlic. Remove some of the outer papery layers. Place garlic heads in a small baking dish. Drizzle with 2 tablespoons of the oil. Roast until the garlic cloves are very tender, about 50 minutes.

When cool enough to handle, squeeze the garlic cloves, which should be quite soft, into a small bowl. Add the oil from the roasting pan. Mash the mixture with a fork.

Heat 1 tablespoon of oil in a heavy medium pot over medium heat. Add onion and cook, stirring occasionally, until it begins to soften, 4 to 5 minutes. Add rosemary, thyme, sugar, and salt to taste. Stir 1 minute then add the tomatoes with juices, broth, bay leaf, and garlic paste. Bring to a simmer. Reduce heat, and cook until onion and tomatoes are very tender, 20 to 30 minutes. Remove bay leaf.

Puree the soup in a food processor or blender to desired consistency. Adjust seasoning, if needed.

Meanwhile, increase oven temperature to 400 degrees.

Toss baguette slices with the remaining 1 tablespoon oil and the grated cheese. Arrange on baking sheet. Bake until toasted, 3 to 4 minutes on each side.

Ladle soup into bowls. Garnish each serving with cheese toasts.

4

The Salad

For a wedding gift, Ken's parents bought us a beautiful wooden salad bowl. Before I used it the first time, I seasoned it with a neutral oil to protect it, carefully rubbing it in and wiping off the excess, turning the wood into a richer dark reddish brown.

Over the years the inside of the bowl has developed an almost silky patina from nothing more than the combining of dozens, if not hundreds, of salads. It wasn't something I tried to achieve. It just happened with time—and lots and lots of tossing.

The beauty of a salad is its individual parts—lettuces, other vegetables, maybe fruits, cheese, and croutons—all held together by some kind of dressing, whether a creamy version or a tart vinaigrette.

I've tossed a lot of things together in my salad bowl, and in my life, too, I suppose. It hasn't all been successful. Some combinations married beautifully, but others didn't make a harmonious meal, with ingredients never quite working as well in reality as they did in my mind's eye.

When Ken and I decided to get married, we chose to buy a home together, one that would be a new start for us and the children, instead of me trying to move into their already-established world.

I had moved dozens of times. But almost always the search for new dwellings was something I did on my own, either looking to move into a house or an apartment that belonged to someone else or finding the place and then looking for a roommate. In the last decade, I had lived completely on my own, from my studio in San Francisco to my first townhouse in Columbus, then my condo in Dublin near Ken and the kids. Searching for a house with someone else in what still felt like a new city to me was a novel experience.

It's hard to compare Dublin, Ohio, to San Francisco. At first glance, it might seem like no comparison at all. San Francisco boasts unique architecture, complete with Victorian houses with bay windows and frilly gingerbread detailing. Because of a limited amount of land, houses are built up, not out, so garages are the first floor with subsequent floors stacked upon one another, either divided into flats or lived in whole as traditional single family homes.

Being surrounded by water on three sides gives the city a unique climate, too. Dense fog is commonplace, making the rare blue-sky days something to celebrate. San Francisco has only two real seasons: rainy months from November to March, and the rest of the year. It might get hot in the East Bay and Marin during summer, and it snows inland in the Sierras in winter, but in San Francisco, most days are damp, foggy, and around fifty degrees.

Don't be fooled, however. The fog cloaks the city in a rare and mysterious beauty that is breathtaking on its worst days.

Columbus, Ohio, on the other hand, is a solid Midwestern city, sturdy and practical. It's a well-made wool blazer to San Francisco's vibrantly colored silk sari. And Dublin is Columbus's pretty sister with manicured lawns and spacious houses, neatly planned developments with stacked rock and brick entryways, and Irish names such as Donegal Cliffs and Tartan Fields.

Ever traditional, Columbus offers the usual four seasons, with something to love in each of them, if it's only the anticipation of the next one to come. Winters tend toward cold and gray with occasional snow. By February, residents long for the rebirth of a spring that never disappoints: first daffodils, then forsythia and dogwoods and cherry trees, with so many blooms that the whole landscape is painted yellow and magenta and white. Residents reach for their flip-flops and shorts too soon, hanging up their winter coats and refusing to get them out again when a warm streak turns into a cold snap.

Summers are hot and sticky, green and lush, with pop-up thunderstorms and brilliant lightening displays. Crickets chirp, and fireflies light the night sky in a mesmerizing visual symphony. The cool of fall brings with it another palate of colors: ruby red, gold, and orange, melding into every possible combination on a single leaf. Autumn air smells wet with the scent of winter breezes not far behind.

Always too soon, each season leaves; but like clockwork, with the tick-tock of a big timepiece no one can see, the seasons return, one after another, year after year.

Ken loves to go through open houses. His Sundays are complete if he can find time to sneak into a couple of them in different neighborhoods, to study the architecture, the design, and how the residents use the space. We were looking at houses just for fun long before we decided to get married. I knew our relationship was becoming more serious when our searches turned from casual walk-throughs to discussions of how we might use a space and if we could see ourselves actually dwelling in a certain house.

After much searching, we found a house we all loved just a few blocks from Ken's current home. It was close to St. Brigid Church, where the children went to school and the family went to Mass. (Later, we could hear the bells announcing Mass each Sunday, and if we heard it other days, we would guess at the occasion. Bells on Saturday likely meant a wedding. The single bell tolling over and over on a weekday meant a funeral. Early morning bells on a weekday meant an all-school Mass.)

The kitchen of the new house was spacious, and it was the focal point of the house, a plus for me. A built-in table attached to the island with the stovetop would work as both our place for meals and as a place for the kids to do homework. It opened into the family room, so everyone could feel connected no matter where they were downstairs.

Ken liked the screened-in patio that promised a place for summer meals, as well as a vantage point from which to watch the birds and wildlife that seemed to abound in the yard's mature trees and bushes.

The kids were happy to know that they would each have their own bedroom, though they had to share a bathroom. It was divided so that one person could shower while the others still had access to the sinks and mirror, which would make bathing, teeth-brushing, and primping possible at the same time.

Ken and the kids moved into the house a few months before we were married. I set up the kitchen, moving in my appliances, pots, pans, and knives. It was my domain from the beginning.

Ken and I took inventory of the rest of our furnishings, deciding what to keep. My living room set was newer—Ken had helped me purchase it when I bought my condo—so we moved that to the new house. But the rest of what I had—an extra bed, a tattered dresser, a too-small dining room table with only four chairs—we didn't need.

Some items moved directly from Ken's old house to the new one, taking up the same place in the new space. A photo of Grace smiling from a ski lodge in Vermont moved from the original living room to the new one, as did a framed article with a photo of the five of them from the University of Dayton alumni magazine. It detailed not only Grace's life, but also how Ken had set up a scholarship at the university in her name after she died.

Wedding photos of Ken and Grace came with us, too, moving from what had been their bedroom to what became ours. A young Grace, radiant in her white lace dress and veil stared at her bouquet of Gerber daisies from a frame on the nightstand. Another picture of her and Ken, superimposed overlooking the altar while appearing to look at each other, expressions full of hope and promise, stood on the bureau.

The photos remained there after Ken and I were married. I wanted Ken to have time to assimilate his grief into our new life, so I said nothing. We both had much to get used to. But as the months drew on, the photos stayed put. I knew he missed her, but I began to feel that he missed her more than he loved me.

These were feelings I didn't feel I could share, not with Ken or with anyone else. I didn't want to appear demanding, as though I wanted all traces of Grace removed. The opposite was actually true: I worked hard at asking Ken questions about Grace, at times purposefully in front of the kids so they would know that talking about their mother was fine with me.

Not only could I not share my feelings about the photos with anyone, I wasn't proud of having them at all. I had a vision of myself being the ultimate caring wife and stepmother, carefree and easygoing, certainly not hung up with petty jealousies about my husband's first wife.

Yet there she was, every day, every night, perpetually young and beautiful. In our bedroom. Over time, it became a knot in my throat that became more difficult to swallow.

About a year after Ken and I were married, I developed a friendship with a young woman at the newspaper where I worked. It was an unlikely alliance that no doubt God had a hand in.

Kristy was fifteen years my junior and perpetually perky and upbeat, in a Katie Couric kind of way, traits I usually find suspect. She moved from news to features to specialize in slice-of-life stories, such as the impact on a family after the father died fighting in Iraq, or the effects on a young woman a year after her fiancé disappeared under mysterious circumstances.

Kristy and I didn't have much reason to interact, but one day she came to me and told me she was setting up a youth team of high school students for the paper. She wanted to get their input on story ideas and also to use them as an avenue to sources that might otherwise be difficult to access.

"Robin, you have kids in high school, don't you?" she asked, stopping by my desk.

"No. Ben's in eighth grade, and the twins are in sixth."

"You have twins?"

"I do. They're my stepdaughters."

"You have stepchildren?" She was keenly interested.

Kristy, it turned out, was about to marry a man who had twin sons that were a year younger than Molly and Sarah, and a daughter a few years younger than the boys. It was like my situation, reversed.

Mike, her husband-to-be, was divorced, and the children's mother was still on the scene, so their scenario wasn't identical to mine. Still, we had so much in common, issues that few others in our lives could really grasp.

Kristy became my ally, my confidant. I could share with her the struggles I had with stepparenting and interactions with Grace's family. She could listen with an understanding no one else possessed, and when she expressed her own challenges, it confirmed to me that I wasn't alone.

"I accept that there are some things I don't get by marrying Mike," Kristy told me one day when we were having lunch together. "I don't get to be his first love. I don't get to have his first child with him. But I get to form my own paths with him, paths that have nothing to do with where he's been or where I've been before now."

There it was. Wisdom I had never put into words. I would never be Ken's first love, either. We wouldn't have that traditional first year of marriage where we could get to know each other through just living together, learning each other's quirks and what buttons not to push—or to push when the situation warranted it—with no one but ourselves and each other to care for or about.

We started our marriage with Ben, Molly, and Sarah—not to mention an extra set of in-laws. I would always share space with Grace in each of their hearts. I would never have wife or mother space all to myself. But while I might not be the first or the only, I could choose to live in the present and not be covered in the shadow of the past.

The photos of Grace remained in our bedroom, but I tried to let them be little more than objects to me. My stony heart started to crack.

Despite a few rough patches in our early days of marriage, I reminded myself often of the signs from God that Ken and I belonged together, reflecting on how we had met, which, in itself, seemed like something of a miracle.

And sometimes, God reminded me himself.

When I moved into the house with Ken and the kids after we were married, I left a big plastic carton of photos in the garage. Ken asked often if he could bring it in and move it to the basement, but I always told him I wanted to go through it first and sort what I could get rid of.

In that first summer, we decided to have a garage sale, and my tub of pictures was taking up precious space. I finally acquiesced for Ken to take it to the basement. He picked it up and looked through the clear lid at the photo on top.

"Why do you have my photo of the chapel?" he asked, looking at the picture from the University of Dayton.

"That's my picture," I told him. "I took it. I've had it since I was in college. But what's it doing on top of all the other photos? I haven't looked at that in years."

Ken said, quite certainly, "I took this photo. I remember the day I took it."

"I remember the day *I* took it," I said, just as sure. "I don't remember taking that one exactly but I remember taking other photos of UD that day."

"It's my picture," Ken said, in a voice with no room for doubt.

"How do you know it's yours?"

"I remember every photo I've taken." Ken makes his living as an engineer, but his passion is photography. He took it up in high school and never stopped, even working as a wedding photographer on weekends after college. His collection of photos is massive, yet he is attached to every one of them.

"Well, why do I have it in my things if it's your photo?" I asked him.

Ken put down the tub and opened the lid. He picked up the photo and turned it over. He handed it to me.

"Do you remember giving this to me?" I asked him, not believing what I saw. Ken shook his head slowly. On the back of the photo was written, "Photo by Ken Heigle," unmistakably in my handwriting, even the misspelling of Ken's last name.

Months later, Ken was cleaning the basement because we were turning it into a television room for the kids for those nights when we didn't all agree on what we wanted to watch. He came up to the kitchen carrying a stack of greeting cards. "Look at this," he said quietly, holding up the cards. I took them from him and started to open the one on the top.

"They're cards I gave Grace over the years," he said, smiling.

I stopped and closed the card, handing the pile back to him. He looked confused.

I pushed down the knot in my throat and swallowed hard. "I don't want to read them," I told him as nicely as I could.

"Why not?"

"I just can't. I don't mind you talking about her. I like it, in fact, learning about her. But, honey, I can't read notes from you telling her how much you loved her."

"I don't understand."

I thought back to my conversations with Kristy and echoed her words. "I accept that I'm not your first love," I told him. "I know that you loved her, that you still love her. But I don't need to read your words to her to know that."

"I would read letters you wrote to old boyfriends," he said.

I sighed. "It's completely different, don't you think?"

"How?"

"Those former boyfriends and I chose not to be together any more. You didn't choose not to be with Grace."

He paused, looking at me. "I don't understand this. I thought it was okay to share this part of my life with you."

"Ken, I've let you share everything. I've never said no to anything. I just can't do this. I have to draw a line here."

"Other things bother you, then?"

"Sometimes . . ."

"What? What else bothers you?" His tone was growing angry.

"The photos," I said. "Your wedding photos in our bedroom."

He looked stricken. "I keep those up for the kids mostly," he said. "They were always up in the bedroom at our old house."

"I know," I answered, feeling the waves of guilt building in my stomach while the childish emotions rushed out. "But I wake up every day and see her, see the two of you, so happy. I wonder how there can be any room in your heart for me."

"It's not the same," he said slowly. "My loving her and missing her have nothing to do with how much I love you. And I love you very much. God gives us hearts big enough for exponential amounts of love."

He gathered me in his arms, and I lay my head against his chest where I could hear his heart beating. *Yes*, I thought, my petty fears evaporating, *There is certainly enough room in this heart of his for boundless love.* I would just have to make sure my own heart wasn't so stony that I couldn't receive that love.

Slowly, over the next few months, the photos in our bedroom came down, and Ken put a photo of Grace in each of the kids' rooms instead. Our house had all kinds of room for love. But sometimes we had to clear space and open doors to make room for all that God was giving us.

The truth is, the five of us together were almost always great from the start. We ate together, prayed together, and lived together as if it had always been this way. I sometimes thought that, had we lived in a void, on a private island, we could have lived conflict-free. But as I toasted at our wedding, I had married into not one family, but two. Juggling them, plus mine, turned out to be one of my greatest challenges.

Ken's parents welcomed me as though I had always been part of the family. And more times than not, when we were together with Ken's siblings and their families, the dynamic was great, although sometimes the sheer volume of people was overwhelming for me—three siblings, plus spouses, eight nieces and nephews, and dozens—literally—of aunts, uncles, and cousins.

With my sister, her husband and children, the family clicked, too. The day before we were married, Sarah said to me, "Do you know what I'm looking forward to most about the wedding?"

"What?" I asked, expecting to hear about her dress or the cake.

"Josh will officially be my cousin." Her words were a testament to family.

Ken's family longed to see their brother and son happy again. For my family, Ken was an addition, not a substitution or replacement.

I knew before we married that our relationship was likely to be difficult for Grace's family. But I thought that, somehow, building a blended family would be easier for me. I did, after all, come from one myself, though I never would have thought to call it that when I was a child.

The only physical fight I ever got into was in the sixth grade when Kelly Hunter told me that my half brothers, who had a different last name from mine, weren't my real brothers. I tackled the much bigger girl and scuffled with her in the dirt of the playground for even suggesting that my family was somehow less than whole or complete.

Perhaps due to the work of my parents or maybe just childish acceptance, I couldn't see a difference between my half brothers, Rick and Scott, and my "full" siblings, Mark and Dorothy. I knew we had different fathers and that Rick's and Scott's dad had died. In the summertime, they would go stay with their father's parents, Leone and Earl, and we would go stay with my father's mother and sister. Then we would all meet at my mother's childhood family home and visit with her family. There was nothing unordinary or strange about any of it.

Holidays were the same. Leone and Earl always came to our house for Thanksgiving and Christmas, as did my grandmother and Aunt Jane. I don't remember strained emotions, tense conversations, or secret battles between any of the adults.

What I hadn't anticipated with my marriage was that living in the shadow of a first wife could sometimes be an uncomfortable place, especially when Grace's family visited. I thought somehow, over time, that the shadow would lighten, and the relationships would ease into a kind of relaxed acceptance. But as the years drew on, the relationships with her family seemed as stilted as they were the first time we met. I always felt like the outsider, the extra.

I grew discouraged and came to dread their visits, painting on a smile, but counting the minutes until they were over.

I found myself missing my parents more than usual, especially my father. "How did you do it?" I wanted to ask him. "What was your secret? Were you uncomfortable with Leone and Earl? Was there really no strain, or did you and Mom just make it look easy?"

Of course, Dad was no longer there to answer.

Slowly my questions to my father, usually uttered in frustration in anticipation of a visit or some other interaction, became something else entirely. Prayers. Daily prayers. Out loud. Usually in the car.

Those prayers became a ray of light. I don't mean that my prayers were answered. In fact, I'd say that as I spoke them at the beginning, they weren't answered at all. But my prayers changed, and my attitude changed.

In the beginning, they were one-sided bitch sessions, a laundry list of what I wanted, or the reliving of a perceived slight. "Why can't this just be easier?" I would say.

It didn't change the situation. It didn't change our relationships. But there was something about my speaking the words out loud over time that changed me. Maybe just speaking my frustrations released me from them. Maybe I heard how selfish my prayers were. After a time, without my really noticing, the prayers changed.

"Please, God, help me to understand all of them better."

Then, "Please, God, help me to have patience with them."

And finally, "Please, God, help me to see them as you see them."

I don't achieve that successfully every day. But when I got to the point where I could start from the basis that we're all God's children and God loves every one (every *single* one, no exceptions), my perception shifted.

And the daily prayers, out loud, on my way to work and sometimes on the way home, changed more than just my dismay about

Grace's family. They became a way to refocus my thoughts from a laundry list of what I wanted, to prayers for those I loved—and even more important, for those I found difficult to love. It turned the light from inward to outward, helping me prioritize my thoughts and plans for the day from the moment I left the sanctuary of my home.

Our extended family dynamic worked on the level it needed to. I was just so entrenched in the minutiae that I often couldn't see it.

When I lived in San Francisco, I developed what felt like a pulled muscle between my eyes, a tightness that often left me rubbing them, trying to refocus. Thinking that I needed glasses, I went to an optometrist.

"Look here," he said, holding a piece of paper with letters close to my eyes, while he sat close, staring at my pupils. "Now here," he said, moving it farther away. "Tell me when it's in focus."

He nodded, and performed a few more tests. "When I move the paper from close up to farther away, your eyes kind of wiggle, shaking back and forth while they try to focus," he said. "Do you do a lot of computer work?"

"I spend most of my day at the computer," I said. Then I remembered I was editing a book for a publishing house in the evenings. "I guess I spend a lot of time on the computer at night, too."

He nodded again. "You don't need glasses. You just need to look up once in a while. Focus on something in the distance."

"Like the mountains?"

He laughed. "Yes, like the mountains. I prescribe that at least once an hour you look up from your computer and find the mountains in the distance. Train your eyes to see not just what's in front of you, but what's a little farther away, too."

For all the stress and discomfort I might feel at a visit from Grace's family, especially when it fell at a milestone event such as the children's confirmation or graduation, I had only to look at the bigger picture, the mountains in the distance, to see that it was all working, at least from the kids' perspective. The families—Grace's, Ken's, and mine—were together, united toward one goal: the happiness of Ben, Molly, and Sarah. Maybe we didn't always agree on how to get there. Maybe we were a lot like the United States: different territories and personalities, different vistas and viewpoints. But united, nonetheless, in purpose, and ultimately, in love.

In the days before I became Catholic, at one of the last sessions of the confirmation rites for adults, Deacon Frank gave us an up-close tour of the altar. He stopped at the crucifix.

At St. Brigid, the crucifix isn't like those of many churches, a large cross with a life-size Jesus hanging on it. It's smaller, more of an art piece. Beside the cross is Mary, with her finger pointing up.

"It's as though she's saying, 'Don't look at me,'" Frank said. "'Look at him.'"

And on the other side is St. John, with his finger on his chin and a scroll under his arm, as though thinking, *What does all this mean?*

"And notice what's on Jesus' head," Frank said, pointing to the crown. "It's not a crown of thorns, but a royal crown, a gold crown."

He continued. "What we have to remember is that becoming Catholic doesn't make us better than anyone else. And it doesn't promise us a life without pain. Jesus doesn't promise us a crown, a halo. That comes later, in heaven. On earth, he only promises a cross. We all have to take up our crosses."

My cross is much like my salad bowl, worn and familiar. It is the opposite of "happily ever after." It is the cross of hard work, suffering, and rebuilding. It is the cross of grace. And I wouldn't trade it for anything.

Warm Goat Cheese Salad

Makes 6 servings

This is one of Ken's favorite salads of mine. When he eats it, he tells me I've spoiled him for eating in restaurants; he likes the food I cook better. For weeknight dinners, I go with something simpler: mixed greens with the same dressing, chopped apples, and crumbled goat cheese. But for a special occasion, it's hard to beat this.

Vinaigrette:

1 teaspoon Dijon mustard

1 teaspoon honey or sugar

2 tablespoons white wine vinegar, fresh lemon juice, or a combination

Kosher salt to taste

Freshly ground pepper to taste

1 tablespoon chopped fresh herbs such as thyme or parsley (optional)

⅓ cup extra-virgin olive oil

Salad:

Nonstick cooking spray

1 large egg

1 tablespoon water

1 cup soft fresh bread crumbs

1 tablespoon chopped fresh thyme

2 logs (6 ounces each) fresh goat cheese, each cut into 6 rounds

Kosher salt and freshly ground pepper to taste

10 cups mixed baby greens

½ cup dried cranberries, raisins, or dried cherries

To make the dressing: Whisk the mustard, honey, vinegar, salt, pepper, and herbs (if using) in a small bowl. Gradually whisk in olive oil.

To make salad: Preheat oven to 400 degrees. Line a baking sheet with foil. Mist with cooking spray.

Whisk egg and water in a shallow bowl. Combine bread crumbs and thyme in another shallow bowl.

Season goat cheese lightly with salt and pepper. Dip in egg mixture, then in bread crumb mixture, coating completely. Arrange on baking sheet.

Bake just until bread crumbs are golden brown and cheese is soft but not melted, 8 to 10 minutes.

Toss greens with some of dressing. Arrange on salad plates. Top each with 2 goat cheese rounds. Sprinkle with dried fruit. Drizzle with remaining dressing and serve immediately.

5
The Bread

The thing about bread is, you can't rush it. You have to give it the right environment with the right touch of warmth and precise ratio of yeast to flour to liquid. But you can't make it become bread any quicker. That just takes time.

My father was an excellent bread baker, which is not really a surprise. He was a chemist, and baking is, after all, a formula before it's an art form. Other cooking would frustrate Dad; my mother made him do all the grilling. He was never quite satisfied with his barbecued pork chops or slabs of ribs that, to him, seemed too saucy or too caramelized.

But later in his life, when I was in high school, he picked up a book on bread baking. He would spend Sundays making white bread or French loaves or, later, pretzels that he would form into everyone's initials. He didn't worry about what he was making. He would follow the recipe meticulously, knowing precisely what would happen at every step. The results were, of course, exactly as he expected.

I am more of a cook than a baker. I can make a good pie and can even make a loaf of bread if necessary, but I lack the diligence and practice required to be truly superior at baking. I like to cook because I can throw things together, fix the flavors midstream if I need to, and usually come out with something delicious. Baking, and life, require a little more patience—something I do not have in abundance.

Somewhere along the way, I decided that if I was going to do this stepmother thing, I was going to do it perfectly. *Perfect* is a dangerous word. It's full of expectations, most of which I've since come to believe aren't based in reality. Perfection as I'd perceived it precluded emptying oneself to become obedient to God's plan. Being perfect takes up an awful lot of space, and so it doesn't allow for that emptying thing to happen.

For me, God's will became supplanted—again—with my own will to be a perfect wife and stepmother. I wanted to be a straight-A mom right out of the chute, like a student in cooking school who wants to be Julia Child the day she graduates. I allowed myself no leeway, no room for learning, or God forbid, mistakes.

I knew, just *knew*, that if I tried harder, worked harder, and loved harder, I would be a perfect straight-A mom. What that search for perfection actually gave me was an A+ bout of anxiety that turned into something more serious.

Not quite a year after we were married, I was sitting at my desk at the newspaper. I felt a flutter in my chest. It wasn't painful, just odd. And it lasted long enough that I thought I was going to pass out. I picked up my cell phone and walked calmly to the stairwell, the only place for at least partial privacy in the bustling cubescape of the newsroom.

Then I coughed. I felt a quiet thump, then my heart rhythm seemed to be restored. What was it? Did I just have a heart attack? But I felt no pain. A stroke? But I was fine now.

A voice inside me said that tightness and shallow breathing were something to check out. I called my physician. When I told the nurse about the cough, she said the episode warranted a visit. A cough is often the body's way to try to correct an abnormal heart rhythm. A few more episodes of what I perceived to be a sputtering heart rate and a trip to the emergency room landed me in the office of a cardiologist.

Ken and I sat quietly while the doctor looked over my EKG and stress test results. Ken's foot jiggled anxiously, and not for the first time since this heart thing had started, I felt guilty. Here was a man who had lost his wife to cancer, and now his new wife of not yet a year was complaining of heart palpitations.

"Your heart is perfectly fine," the cardiologist said, after reviewing my test results. "Some women in their forties"—I loved the as-you-age comment—"experience what they think are unusual rhythms, but they're nothing to worry about."

Then he said it was possible I was just anxious. "Is there anything that could be causing you stress?" he asked.

"Like a new marriage and three stepchildren?" I wanted to say but didn't. I left with a clean bill of health, promising him and my husband that I would just try to relax.

Of course, relaxing wasn't something I had mastered exactly. When I lived in San Francisco, I juggled multiple projects constantly—consulting and editing books in addition to my full-time plus restaurant critic/food writing job—all in the name of bettering my career.

Every year, the consulting firm for which I did work on the side threw a cocktail party to thank the chef's council, a group of us who helped food companies brainstorm and create new products. It was sensational work, highly creative, focused, and short-term. It also paid what I considered to be a huge amount of money, so I felt the need to go all out for every project.

At the party, I ran into one of my teachers from cooking school, someone who also consulted frequently and whom I occasionally took with me on restaurant reviews. When she asked how I was, I started rattling off every project I had in the works.

She stared at me. "Robin, whenever I'm around you, I expect to see smoke start pouring out of your ears. You're always in overdrive. Slow down. You're going to burn out."

And that was years before I tried to become a super stepmom. The stress I created professionally, then personally, did eventually catch up to me, breaking my healthy heart, though not physically.

After being married about three years, after the newness of my life had worn off but the daily demands and challenges remained, I started to crack. I often found myself crying, though only when no one was looking: after Ken had fallen asleep, when I was in the shower, or driving to and from work. A lifelong insomniac, my sleeplessness reached epic proportions. I would lie awake for hours each night, recounting the day and replaying and analyzing each event.

Then the crying started to creep into less private places such as the dinner table or while watching television. I didn't know why I was crying. I had the perfect life, a job I loved, a husband I loved who adored me, and three beautiful stepchildren who had welcomed me so openly into their lives. Obviously, if the problem wasn't these people close to me, then it had to be me. And if it was me, then I just needed to try harder.

On those nights when I started to cry in bed after Ken went to sleep, I tried to pray, much like the prayers I said after my father died. "Please. Please. Please." The tears dripped down my cheeks as I tried to lie as still as possible and not let my crying turn into actual sobs that would wake Ken.

Inevitably I would feel God come to me. Sometimes I envisioned Jesus sitting on the edge of the bed, and when it was really bad, I felt his arms around me. "What do you want me to do?" I asked silently. But I felt his arms around me, that's all. I couldn't hear him, because the rumblings in my head were so loud.

"Just try harder," I shouted at myself. "Just be better!" It was hard to hear what Jesus might be saying to me when I was so busy screaming at myself.

What I didn't know then was that marriage and parenthood aren't always happy and harmonious. Despite the children's love for me, I often felt fake and disconnected. Somewhere along the way, I had picked up the idea of what a super stepmom would be: a perfect replacement mom with all the right answers, calm and unshakable, and still even a little bit hip and cool. But what I saw when I looked in the mirror was a tense and uptight woman with crow's feet around her eyes, fine lines that were beginning to turn into canyons from my constant frowning and scowling. I may have been trying to be Maria Von Trapp, but I was closer to being the Baroness, cold and remote, uncomfortable and artificial.

I didn't have any good role models. My mother had faced a multitude of heartbreaks, from her own mother dying when she was in college to the tragic death of her first husband, then to losing herself in alcoholism. As a guide, she was dubious. At that time, I wasn't strong enough in my faith to look to Mary, something I often do now.

I had arrived in this land of stepparenting as though landing in a foreign country without a road map or dictionary of the language. I looked around to see what the locals were doing and tried to blend in. The problem was, I didn't believe that I was like the locals. The vast majority of the women I met in Dublin, Ohio—who invariably were the mothers of the kids' friends—were biological parents.

One Christmas, I hosted a mother-daughter cookie exchange. As the mothers sat around the kitchen table nibbling on the sweet treats while the girls played in the finished basement, I felt sort of left out of the conversation. Not shut out—these women were kind and gracious—but left out. The talk centered on school and church and whatever the kids were involved in. Nothing about arts, culture, politics, or worldviews or even personal growth.

As I listened and looked around, it dawned on me that not one of these women worked outside the home. They led what appeared to be perfect lives: beautiful houses always meticulously maintained. They volunteered at their children's schools and were always impeccably dressed at their husbands' sides at all the right events. The kids, the house, the marriage—these formed the totality of their day-to-day lives.

They all seemed happy. But their life was not mine. It wasn't where I was or where I would ever go. I needed my job, my career, in addition to my family. If these neighbors were my role models, then I was in serious trouble because I was already different. Not just different, but lacking in the perfection I held as my ultimate standard.

So the crying continued, starting earlier in the evening and awaking me any night I might actually grab a few hours of sleep.

After work one evening, I climbed into my car in the parking lot and immediately started sobbing. "What is this?" I cried at the car's interior. The day hadn't been bad at work; in fact, I was managing work beautifully, even though a television gig had recently been added to my responsibilities as food editor. Once a week, I taped a cooking segment with the local news station to air in conjunction with that week's Food section. It was a whole new realm for me, requiring a new set of skills. It was stressful, I suppose, but I had managed so much more in San Francisco between my full-time job and freelance work. If work was OK, then why was I sitting in my car in the parking lot sobbing?

Then it dawned on me. I was crying because it was time to go home.

I was leaving the land of deadlines and demanding bosses and a constantly expanding workload to go into the abyss: my home life. Where three little people needed guidance and structure and love—in addition to being dropped off and picked up and helped with their homework. Dinner needed to be made, dishes washed, and piles of laundry washed and put away. I could look around the house and find a dozen or more projects that needed tending to *every night*.

And it flattened me.

Let me step back for a moment and explain that the division of household labor came naturally to Ken and me; we both just did what we were best at. Of course, cooking went to me, just as mowing the lawn and shoveling the snow went to Ken. (I had lived in California so long I'd never had to learn to do either.) I'd done laundry my whole life, so I could take that over fine—though the volume of laundry for five people compared to one was more than a little daunting.

The housework? We split it. But living alone for so long had left me comfortable with a certain degree of mess. Which is to say, not much. When I lived alone, there wasn't much mess because there was just me. Add three kids and a husband making their own little messes, and suddenly it's a much bigger mess.

The smooth clean lines of a demanding job didn't unhinge me because I knew what was expected and how to accomplish it. I was in control. At home? It was messy and sticky and constantly changing. I struggled with getting the kids to choose fruits and vegetables over sweets. I worried that Ben wasn't studying enough and that the girls were studying too much. I feared that I wasn't making Ken happy because I constantly harped on the state of the house, which no matter how hard I tried, always seem to be accumulating dust and trash and piles—and piles—of laundry.

I could say in my head that these things didn't matter, that a life and a marriage aren't judged by the cleanliness of a house or how many veggies your kids eat. But my heart had grown stony and wouldn't listen.

Between sobs, I called my sister. "I don't know what's wrong with me. I don't know why I'm so sad. I don't know why this isn't easier. It's been three years. I mean, come on! Why am I still struggling with their schedules and laundry and piles of dishes? Why am I undone by *that*?"

Dorothy murmured and tried to comfort me, but I was inconsolable.

"Maybe," I said, unsure I wanted to say what I had been thinking for weeks, "I need help."

"I think it's a good idea," Dorothy said, having watched me descend into this sad muck for months.

My crying stopped, and I had a sense that maybe all this internal struggle was more visible on the outside than I'd realized.

"Robin," she went on, "I'm sure you could handle this on your own. But if you knew you could do something that would make it better sooner, wouldn't you want to do it? If you were sick with an infection that would probably clear up on its own, but there was a drug that would make you well sooner, you'd take it, right?"

Dorothy had endured her own anxiety crisis a year before when she was pregnant with her second child. She, too, found herself crying constantly, finding little joy in caring for Josh or anything else.

It was her fear of what this stress was doing to her unborn baby that finally led her to get professional help, which made an enormous difference, and fairly quickly.

She sent me an e-mail with her counselor's phone number. I made the call when I got home that night, leaving a message something like this: "I'm not sure why I'm calling. There's nothing really wrong. I just can't seem to stop crying." Pause, tears welling up. "I cry all the time."

My first appointment with Julie was much the same. I cried. And cried. The only words I could get out were, "I don't know why I'm crying. I have everything I could ever want." Over the next few sessions I was able to explain to her how hard I tried at being a good wife and mother, but how I actually felt like a fake.

When Ben started high school, I went grudgingly to the mother's club meeting. Grudgingly because I didn't feel like I belonged. A woman who went to our church, whose youngest daughter was a senior came up to me and touched my arm. "I just want you to know how beautifully you've taken to all of this," she said.

"All of this?" I asked. I wondered if she meant the mother's club, where I had wandered from table to table holding my watered down Dixie Cup of Hi-C, wondering whether I should sign up for the fashion show or the garden committee, hoping to find something as simple—and private—as a bake sale.

"Motherhood. I see you all together, and you're a family. You've jumped right in."

I'd jumped right in, all right. But most days I felt like I was sinking, not swimming. Apparently I made it look good, because I received a lot of comments similar to this woman's.

"I see you at church together, and I just cry," said a woman who had known Ken and Grace. "I used to cry because it broke my heart to see the four of them. Now, when I see the five of you, I'm so happy."

An older woman at church who was friends with Grace's mother came up to me at church every so often and whispered, "You are so amazing."

What I felt like was a great imposter. "Today, the role of Ben, Molly, and Sarah's mother will be played by Robin Davis, the understudy." Too bad no one ever gave me the script, and that I didn't know my lines.

"So why don't you tell them?" Julie asked, after I'd described this life I had created.

"Tell them what?"

"Tell them it's hard. Tell them you're struggling. When someone asks, even casually, 'How are you?' tell them you're having a hard day."

Was it possible that I was feeling fake because I was acting fake? What would happen if I just stopped trying to be perfect?

The counseling gave me great comfort, helping me put into words and say out loud what was festering in my heart. And Julie was able to sort my feelings and put together actions to bring me out of this darkness.

Still, it wasn't an easy transition. I had fallen into what Julie called a "major depressive episode." I couldn't assimilate who I thought I should be and who I believed I actually was. Since I'd entered this marriage I had carefully scripted everything in my head. But nothing was going according to my plans. It wasn't getting easier. I wasn't feeling more comfortable in this life.

"Have you always planned your life this carefully?" Julie asked me.

I thought for a moment about how I had left Dayton and my family—and God—almost out of spite, and how I had determinedly put myself through cooking school, how I had carefully constructed what I thought would be a "perfect life" only to discover it wasn't what I wanted at all. "Yes," I told Julie. "I always have a plan and a plan B and C and D."

"And how has that worked out for you?"

Looking at my life at that moment, I had to admit, it wasn't going well.

"You need to live in the moment, not rehearse the future," Julie told me. "When you try to live in the future, you're destined for disappointment. Life will never be exactly the way you imagine it."

There was one more thing I had to do. "You need to tell Ben, Molly, and Sarah," she said.

"Tell them I'm depressed?"

"Be honest with them," she said. "Ken was always honest with them about their mother's illness. You've both been honest with them about your relationship. Now it's time to be honest with them about *you*."

After dinner one night, I asked them to stay around the table. "I want to tell you something." I took a deep breath and started on the part I had practiced. "When Josh was a baby, I used to tell him all the time when I watched him, when I changed his diaper, 'Be nice to me, Josh. Your Aunt Robin doesn't really know what she's doing.'"

I looked around at my three stepchildren. "I don't really know what I'm doing with you guys, either," I said. "I've been trying hard to be perfect—whatever that means—and I haven't been doing a very good job. I've become really sad. So I've been seeing a kind of doctor. The doctor says I'm depressed. Have you heard that word before?"

They nodded. "Is that why you cry?" Sarah asked.

"It is. And I want you to know that it's not you, none of you. I just haven't been really sure what it is I'm supposed to be doing, and

I became convinced I wasn't doing it right. But I'm working on it, OK? And I believe I'll get better."

Ben looked relieved. He smiled at me. "What can we do?"

Tears welled up in my eyes. Such a big heart, this boy. "Nothing," I told him. "Just be you. And pray for me."

The kids went off to do their homework, and I sat at the table and looked at Ken. "How do you feel?" he asked.

"About a hundred pounds lighter."

"They don't expect you to be perfect. They love you just the way you are."

And I knew, maybe for the first time, that it was true. But it wasn't just a flip of a switch: click, I was better. I still struggled often with my role, sometimes losing sight of who I was trying to be and who I actually was.

I usually let Ken take the lead in most things concerning the kids. I always figured he knew better. But every so often, I'd recognize there were other paths than the one he put them on.

Take math, for instance. When Ben was in seventh grade, Ken pushed him to excel in math. St. Brigid offered algebra in eighth grade, but students had to pass a test to get into it. Ken worked through problems every night with Ben at the kitchen table while I made dinner; Ben wasn't always enthusiastic about the process.

"If you take algebra in eighth grade, then you can take geometry as a freshman, trigonometry as a sophomore, calculus as a junior, and AP calculus as a senior," Ken said, explaining, again, why this extra studying was necessary. "It's very important to take calculus before college. You'll be better prepared."

I drained a pot of pasta, then dumped it into a skillet where onions and garlic had been cooking. I added peas, then a little Parmesan, last minute touches for dinner, all the while listening to the exchange at the table, one I had heard a few times before.

I believed what Ken said: Math was important. And I knew that if Ben went through calculus in high school, he would probably have an easier time with any math classes he had to take in college.

But I also knew something else. "Some people go their whole lives without taking calculus," I said quietly. Ken and Ben looked up from the math problems.

"You never took calculus?" they said almost in unison.

I shook my head.

"Never?" Ken said.

"Nope," I replied. "I took algebra in high school and barely squeaked by. I took it again in summer school at college just to prove to myself I could do it. But," I continued excitedly, "I took a six credit-hour class in Shakespeare in college. Now that was awesome."

Ben scrunched up his face. "I'll stick with algebra, I think."

"As long as you know you have choices."

With the girls, the revelation came with dance. Sarah and Molly were taking dance classes before I met them, another opportunity Ken wanted to provide for them, much like soccer and piano lessons.

Molly quickly limited her dance to tumbling, for which she had a natural affinity. She seemed to fly and flip as easily as breathing, even as she became taller. As a high school cheerleader, at 5 foot, 8 inches, she was hard to miss when she took off doing back hand-springs down the field or court, each one more perfect than the last.

Sarah tried tumbling, too, but became frustrated when it didn't come as easily to her as it did to Molly. "I think you should try ballet," Ken told her.

"Ballet?" Sarah groaned. "It's so boring."

Sarah had taken hip-hop and tap, but never ballet. Between sixth and seventh grade, we convinced her to try it. She grudgingly agreed, mostly because it was just for a few weeks during the summer.

She took to the classical dance form the way Molly had taken to tumbling. She jumped levels quickly and worked diligently, and by her freshman year in high school, she was on pointe and dancing fifteen hours a week or more.

Ken and I supported her dance, sending her to a summer intensive program in Cincinnati for three weeks after her freshman year. Ken wasn't sold on it, but thought living away from home for a short period of time would be good prep for college. At the beginning of her sophomore year, Sarah started talking about going to an extreme ballet camp at Kaatsbaan, an exclusive dance center in Tivoli, New York.

Ken was hesitant. Was this the best way she could be spending her summer? he wondered to me.

"It's so expensive," he told Sarah. "If you really want to go, you'll need to come up with half the money." Instead of being discouraged, Sarah was determined, choosing babysitting jobs over evenings out with friends.

After her three weeks in the Hudson Valley, Sarah was no less in love with dance. Two girls at her studio had declared they were going to major in dance in college, and both were scouring the country, researching dance programs that emphasized ballet, and scheduling their auditions. Sarah talked about them wistfully, with great admiration. "I wish I could do that."

But she knew that as much as Ken supported her dancing, he had subconsciously drawn the line at college, and I followed along. "You have to major in something practical," Ken would say. "You could always minor in dance."

I would chime in with how hard a dancer's life is. "It's so competitive," I would tell her. "You'd work hard, probably waiting tables to support yourself, and maybe never get the opportunity to really dance."

Sarah never fought our opinions, obediently believing what we told her. But sometimes when I drove her and her friends somewhere, I would hear her say how much she loved dance and how she wished she could dance forever.

About the same time, a woman at church approached me after Mass one Sunday. "Robin, I was wondering if you might talk to my daughter," she said. "She just graduated from college and is thinking about doing a writing program in England. Since you're a writer, I thought maybe it would help if you talked to her."

"I'd be happy to," I said. "Have her call me at work."

A few days later she did. "How did you become a writer?" she asked.

"I've been writing since I was about five," I told her. "But for a long time, I didn't know what I wanted to write about." I told her my winding career tale, about graduating from college and moving to California, quitting a good job in marketing and going to cooking school in San Francisco, and finally combining my love of food and my love of writing. It wasn't a straight path, I told her, but I'd always gotten by and had never been unhappy with my choices.

"Do you love to write?" I asked her.

"I do," she said. "But my parents think I need to do something more practical."

I looked at the framed wedding picture on my desk, at Sarah's smiling face. Hadn't Ken and I said the same thing to her? I spun my chair in the other direction, facing away from my desk and the photo. "You should do what you love," I told her. "If you can afford it, go to England. Work office jobs or wait tables if you need to, to support yourself. Start a blog. Take a job in PR or in advertising. But as long as you have the dream, follow it."

Sarah's studio had a meeting with parents of students in the senior intensive program, their most serious dancers. Ken did most parent meetings, but I opted to go to this one. The instructors told us that if our daughters wanted to proceed to a college level or professional dance program, we needed to declare it to the studio so the instructors could make sure they were helping them get to that level.

As we were driving home that night, I asked Sarah, "Do you love to dance?"

"Yes," she told me. "More than anything."

"Then maybe we should start looking at colleges with dance majors."

She looked at me, shocked. "What about Dad?"

"Well, I think we should tell him. Don't you?" I smiled.

That night, when we walked into the house, Ken was watching television. "Ken, Sarah has something she'd like to tell you," I said. Ken turned off the TV and looked at her.

"I want to major in dance in college."

He looked at me. I nodded just slightly. "OK," he said. "What do we need to do?"

Later that night, after she'd gone to bed, he said, "I always wanted to support Sarah in dance, but I guess I didn't think it would last all the way to college. Did you?"

"Not really. But you know I talked to Missy's daughter about writing the other day?"

"Yes."

"I was telling her my story, about finding my way trying to be a writer, then a food writer. I kept telling her she should follow her dream. But I realized that's not what we were saying to Sarah."

He nodded.

"I know it's not practical," I told him. "But if I'd always done what was practical, I never would have met you. We have to make it OK for the kids to take risks and know that God will put them where he wants them to be."

Ken smiled and pulled me into his arms. "Who knew an English major could be so smart?"

Maybe, just maybe, I did have something more than food to offer these kids. Maybe my life—maybe just *me*—was a kind of food for them, too.

Bread Sticks (and Pizza Dough)

Makes about 12 sticks or 4 individual-size pizzas

Pizza is a staple at our house. Columbus has dozens of decent pizzerias, but when time permits, I like to make my own pizza dough. The kids like to stretch and shape the dough, and top it exactly as they like. The recipe also works great as soft warm bread sticks. Serve them with a dipping sauce of good-quality olive oil sprinkled with salt, a pinch of red pepper flakes, and freshly grated Parmesan cheese.

1 envelope active dry yeast

½ cup plus 1 tablespoon warm water (105 to 110 degrees)

1 cup all-purpose flour

½ cup whole wheat flour

1 teaspoon kosher salt

2 teaspoons honey

1 tablespoon extra-virgin olive oil plus additional for coating

Dissolve the yeast in warm water. Let stand 5 to 10 minutes or until foamy.

Combine both flours and salt in a large mixing bowl. Make a well in the center.

Add the honey and 1 tablespoon oil to the yeast mixture. Stir until the honey dissolves. Pour into the well in the flour mixture. Using a wooden spoon, stir to combine. Turn out the dough on a lightly oiled surface. Knead with oiled hands until dough is smooth and still slightly tacky, about 5 minutes.

Lightly oil a large bowl. Place dough in bowl. Turn to coat. Cover bowl with plastic. Let rise in a warm place until doubled in volume, about 1½ to 2 hours.

Punch down dough. Cut into 12 equal pieces (or 4 pieces if making pizzas). Roll the 12 pieces into logs (or the 4 pieces into balls). Place on an ungreased rimmed baking sheet. Cover with a clean kitchen towel. Let rise until doubled in volume, about 45 minutes to an hour.

Preheat oven to 450 degrees. (If making pizza, place a pizza stone in the oven. If you don't have a pizza stone, turn a rimmed baking sheet upside down and place it in the oven.)

If making bread sticks, brush sticks lightly with olive oil. If desired, sprinkle with sea salt, dried Italian seasoning, red pepper flakes, and black pepper. Bake bread sticks until golden brown, 8 to 10 minutes.

If making pizzas, stretch out to four 8-inch rounds. Top as desired. Bake on pizza stone or on the inverted baking sheet until crust is golden brown and topping is bubbly, about 8 to 10 minutes.

6

The Main Course

At a celebratory meal, excess can be a sign of grandeur and well-being.

I remember going to a Chinese wedding for one of the photographers at the *San Francisco Chronicle*. Course after course came out of the kitchen of the banquet hall in Chinatown in what seemed a never-ending stream of food, from crab soup to roast suckling pig, whole steamed fish and Peking duck to red-bean paste-filled steamed buns. Guests—especially those like me who didn't know the tradition of serving far more food than everyone could eat as a sign of good fortune—left groaning from fullness.

But in everyday life, it is the main course that matters most. If everything else from the soup to the salad and bread went away, the entrée, the sustenance, would be enough.

For me and for my family, the main course is our faith.

On our second date, at an event at the country club that would eventually be the site of our wedding reception, I asked Ken if he was ever angry that Grace had died.

"No. I never asked 'why me.' I just sort of thought, 'why not me?' I mean, why should my life be spared pain? What makes me so special?"

I tried to take in what he had said. It was clear that he didn't have an ounce of bitterness about this cruelty life had thrown at him.

Later, on another date, in another deep conversation that we seemed to fall into so easily, I asked more pointedly, "You were *never* mad at God that Grace died?" I remembered my own feelings after my mother died.

"No," Ken said.

"Did you pray for her to be healed? Did you ask him to spare you and the kids this pain?"

"I prayed for strength." He paused for a moment. "He always gave me that, in so many ways. When Grace was in hospice, she stabilized. The doctors told me I had to think about bringing her home. I couldn't imagine having her die at home. I mean, would we be able to live in the house after she died? Would we be able to take that?

"But when Grace asked to come home, I knew at that moment what I had to do. And I knew God would give me the strength to do it." In his darkest moment, Ken had felt God's presence, literally, physically. In the moments when Grace was being taken from him, grace was being given to him in the form of peace and strength.

And hadn't it been the same for me? I had run from God, from everything, but still he was there. He never left my side, though I had refused to acknowledge him. And here he was now, still waiting.

On yet another night, I asked Ken, "How do you pray? Do you have certain prayers you say?"

"No, not certain prayers. I don't really pray the rosary or anything like that. But when Grace was sick, I learned to pray quickly and often. Even now I can get into a meditative state just like that," he said, snapping his fingers.

I wondered if I'd ever prayed like that. I wondered if I'd ever had that kind of communion with God. At that moment I realized that I wanted to. From then on, my whisper prayers began to turn into real prayers, focused prayers, if only occasional. Beginner prayers, I'm sure, with a list of needs and not much listening, but prayers nonetheless. I was no longer being nudged along on my faith journey, but was ready to take steps of my own, for the second time in my life.

After the Sunday school fiasco of my youth, I didn't go back to church again until I was a teenager, and then it was by my own doing, not my parents'. I became active in Fellowship of Christian Athletes (FCA), held Wednesday nights in the home of the pastor of the local Methodist Church.

Frankly, I went because the popular kids went: the football players and cheerleaders. Most of them were my friends, though I always felt I was on the periphery of true popularity, whatever that meant.

But by default, I did establish a kind of relationship with God. FCA meetings started with Scripture and led to discussions about how we could interpret and apply the readings to our lives. It gave me a kind of framework for trying to live a good life, and it led me to believe that if I lived a good life, nothing really bad would happen.

One of the boys told the group that he had never been baptized as a child, so he was going to be baptized on an upcoming Sunday evening. We were all invited, and a group of us attended. While we waited for the service to begin, I read through the readings about baptism. Jeff was being baptized as an adult, but it struck me that my own baptism had been done at my parents' request when I was an infant—and the liturgy made clear that my parents were responsible for my faith formation.

In the weeks following Jeff's baptism, I kept thinking about that covenant and what it truly meant. My parents didn't take me to church. We didn't pray at home. We never talked about God at all. In my sixteen-year-old mind-set—which seemed perpetually perturbed at my parents—they had failed me. It was time to take my faith into my own hands.

I attended the Methodist church most Sundays because Mr. Rebok, the adult supervisor to FCA, was the assistant pastor and some of the other kids from FCA attended there. After services one Sunday, I asked Mr. Rebok if he would baptize me. He agreed, and we set a date.

That sounds noble enough, but this next part I'm not proud of.

I told my mother I was going to be baptized.

"You've already been baptized," she said.

"I know, but we never went to church," I said. Then boldly, "I don't think you and Dad kept up your part of the deal."

My mother just stared at me, registering no emotion. "OK," she said finally. I could detect no real reaction from her. But I can imagine that it must have felt like a slap in the face, a condemnation of her mothering.

"Do you want Dad and me to come?" she asked.

"It's not necessary." I waved her off, not even bothering to turn around. I'm pretty sure one of the reasons I chose for so long not to have children is that I knew firsthand the cruelty they were capable of. I wasn't sure I could have stood up to the kind of withering scorn I threw at my mother that day.

At the time, I held up my second baptism as a pillar of my faith, but it's a memory that still leaves a shameful bitter taste in my mouth. Even if there may have been some merit to my thoughts, I wasn't baptized by my own volition with completely pure intentions. I used it, in part, as a way to judge my parents.

If there's a silver lining to the story, it's that my parents did start taking my sister to church not long after my second baptism. Was it a preventative measure? Did they hope that by doing so they wouldn't go through with my sister what they had gone through with me? Was it guilt? I'll never know.

As an adult, some twenty years later, the first step in my new faith formation was deciding what to do about church. Few of my friends in California went to church. Those that admitted to a spiritual side at all felt they could commune with God in nature just as well as in a building. But I felt that I needed the structure of church, the regularity of services to strengthen my resurrected faith.

Ken and the kids always went to Mass, usually at St. Brigid. It made sense for me to start there. St. Brigid is an expansive church, built into the shape of a cross with a center aisle and two arms off either side. These arms end with stained glass windows depicting sun and water, and slats in the form of crosses separate the panes. Heavy wooden beams line the vaulted ceiling, and a mural of a young Jesus gathering lambs is painted above where the small crucifix hangs.

The first Mass I attended at St. Brigid was the children's Christmas Mass, probably the most attended Mass of the entire year. The children sang with the youth choir, and Ben had a solo. Not only was the church filled to capacity, but several rows of people packed into the vestibule.

It made sense that I start my search for a church during Christmas, the season that revolves around new life. But if I expected this first Mass to be some kind of "aha" moment, in which I would know with certainty that this was the church for me, then the event itself quickly relieved me of that expectation. In fact, I didn't hear much of the Mass, because I was distracted.

I knew that Ken would be sitting with Grace's parents, and we hadn't yet told them we were dating. I asked my sister and nephew, Josh, then eighteen months old, to come with me. We arrived too late to squeeze into the pews with Ken, Pat, and Jim, which was just as well. Josh had recently learned to walk, so sitting for any length of time, especially through a holiday church service, was out of the question. Dorothy and I ended up parking ourselves on the stairs leading to the undercroft, letting Josh toddle up the stairs, then slide back down. We listened as best we could to the Mass coming through the speakers, catching a few notes of Ben's singing and a handful of lines from the homily.

That Mass didn't make me decide right then to become Catholic, but it encouraged me to begin in earnest to discover more about the Catholic Church.

Since my days at the University of Dayton, I had been drawn to the Catholic faith. I loved the grandness and the traditions. I loved that each step of the Mass had meaning and thousands of years of history behind it. And I loved the idea that at the same moment a person celebrated Mass in one corner of the world, millions of others around the globe were celebrating it exactly the same way. That sense of community in the broadest sense was awe-inspiring.

But what about aspects of the church I didn't like? What about the recent sex-abuse scandal? What about the limited possibilities for women in the church? What about the church's stance on gay rights, which was particularly hard for me to accept because I had so many gay friends?

I researched other Protestant churches, looking into their histories and philosophies, hoping to find one that would call to me without reservation. But I never found one I was as drawn to the way I was to Catholicism.

My office at the newspaper is in downtown Columbus, about a block away from St. Joseph Cathedral. I began to spend my lunch hours by going to Mass there and spending time afterward reflecting quietly in the pew.

Noontime Mass is generally quick to accommodate the lunchtime participants. At St. Joseph, one of the priests—whom I nicknamed Fr. Lickety-split—gave homilies so short they could almost fit into a text message. The other regular celebrant spoke as though he had marbles in his mouth, so I took to thinking of him as Fr. Mumbles.

But over time I felt a sense of comfort dedicating my lunch hour to this discovery, and a sense of community with all the regulars who attended, even the quirkier ones: the woman who never used the kneeler but kneeled upon the hard stone floor instead; the businessman who always came late and left right after communion; the homeless man who went last to communion and finished the wine—and no one stopped him from doing so, even though his reasons for drinking the wine may not have been strictly spiritual.

One afternoon I met Ken for lunch but set the time a half hour later than was usual for our lunch dates. "I went to Mass," I told him, as I slid into the booth at a steakhouse not far from my office.

"Today?"

"Just now."

He looked at me, waiting for the next line, the explanation, or, as it turned out, the question. "So how do you reconcile some of the things about the church that you don't agree with?" I asked him.

"Like what?"

"Like that women can't be priests. And the sex-abuse scandal that was covered up."

"The church isn't perfect, Robin," he said. "No one is happy about the sex-abuse scandal. No one." He looked at me more carefully. "What is this about?"

"I'm thinking of becoming Catholic."

"Because of me?"

"Because of me," I said. "I've always been drawn to the church. I've been looking at other churches, too, but I keep coming back to Catholicism."

"You don't have to become Catholic because of our relationship," he said. "I love you even if you're not part of any church."

"I know. But I want to feel that connection. I want to finally be part of a church, for real, completely. I'm just not sure what to do about the parts I don't like."

"Pray about it," Ken said.

I took his advice. A few weeks later, I called Deacon Frank, who headed up the adult initiation program at St. Brigid. He knew Ken and the kids; his youngest daughter was Ben's age. He was one of the four clergy who presided over Grace's funeral Mass. Frank explained that the Rite of Christian Initiation for Adults starts with what's known as inquiry: a time for people interested in becoming Catholic to learn about it and ask questions. He encouraged me to come.

The first night I took a seat in the undercroft next to a woman with long red hair. "I never got around to getting confirmed," she told me, after saying hello. "So I thought I should do that before my kids do. What are you in for?" she joked.

"I'm just thinking of becoming Catholic," I said. "My fiancé is Catholic."

"Oh, you want to have a Catholic wedding. I see."

That wasn't it at all, but I didn't have the words to describe why I was there, that it was just a feeling that this was something I needed to do.

Frank stood next to a small table that had a lit candle flickering on it. "There are a lot of reasons you're all here," he said. "Maybe a friend convinced you to come. Maybe a spouse. Maybe you're tired of your kids tripping over you as they leave the pew for communion each week. But there's another reason you're here that you may not realize." He took a moment to meet each of our gazes. "You're here because Jesus wants you here."

He held up the candle. "If you don't know this already, you'll learn that Catholics are big on things we can see, hear, and touch." He smiled. "This candle is the light of Christ. He knows who you are. Jesus wants you here."

In the weeks that followed, Frank explained many things about the church, many of which I already knew. But he addressed others that troubled me, such as the sex abuse scandal that had broken out in recent years.

"I'm embarrassed," he told us, his voice quivering with anger. "I'm saddened for the church. Nothing is perfect," he said, echoing the words Ken had said to me. "This trouble will cause some people to leave the church. But remember the Gospel of John: after Jesus told the crowds that the only way to the Father was through him, people were leaving Jesus like crazy. He asked the apostles, 'Will you leave, too?' and they replied, 'Where would we go?'"

"The church will survive," Frank said. "God always draws us back."

After the inquiry period, I decided to continue. I met with the other participants in the RCIA process on Thursday nights and attended dismissals after the Gospel each Sunday, in which we again went to the undercroft and discussed the readings, while others at Mass received communion.

In our last meeting before Christmas, Frank gathered us in the Blessed Sacrament Chapel, a small room off the vestibule at St. Brigid that housed the Eucharist and where daily Mass was held. He gave each of us a piece of paper. "If you could change one thing about your life, what would it be?" he asked, instructing us to write it on the paper.

What was holding me back? I wondered. What was keeping me from being happy? I wrote, "I wish I didn't fight God's plan for me."

Frank gathered up the papers and put them in a rough-hewn pottery bowl in the center of the room. Then he told us the story from the Gospel of John about the woman caught in adultery. "They brought her to Jesus in the temple and wanted him to condemn and stone her," Frank said. "But Jesus bent down and wrote in the dust, the ashes of the earth. When they pushed him further, he stood and told them that whoever was without sin could cast the first stone. Then he continued drawing in the dirt.

"When he stood again, the woman was alone. He said, 'No one condemned you?' She answered, 'No one.' And Jesus said, 'Neither do I. Go and sin no more.'"

The detail that was particularly interesting in this story, Frank pointed out, was why Jesus wrote in the dirt. Why did he do that? What was so important about it that the writer thought it should be included in the story?

We discussed it but came up without an answer. In the meantime, Frank struck a match and lit the papers we had given him, the papers on which we had written our fears and secrets. We grew silent as we watched them burn. When the flames went out, Frank stirred the ashes, then held the bowl so that we could look inside it.

"This is what Jesus was drawing in," he said. "He was looking at our sins, our weaknesses, pushing them around, seeing everything. But still, he forgives us."

In the end, I became Catholic because of what the church means to me, and in spite of the aspects of the church that still cause me to struggle.

Catholicism is the tradition in which I believe I can best practice my faith. The word "practice" is key. I will likely never understand all the mysteries completely. I certainly will not agree with everyone who calls themselves Catholic. And I may never hear God speak to me clearly. But I can practice. I can make that daily commitment, not just on Sundays or holidays, and not just when I feel like sending up a whisper prayer to whomever in the universe might be listening.

Despite the conflict within the church, I see so much good: nuns and priests bringing hope to hopeless situations around the world; deacons teaching how God and Scripture and the church are still relevant today; the church's condemnation of war and its prayers for peace. In the Catholic schools that Ben, Molly, and Sarah attended, I saw the call to service, not just for mandatory eighth-grade confirmation and sophomore projects, but also in nonmandated food drives, clothing drives, and the "Christmas on Campus" program that provided joy and gifts to underprivileged children.

I saw believers in church not just on Christmas and Easter, but every Sunday and on nonobligatory days such as Ash Wednesday and Good Friday. My heart still swells every year at the packed pews at St. Brigid on Good Friday at 3:00 p.m. for the Veneration of the Cross. Not just the old parishioners but the new, the young, and entire families file in for the most humbling and somber of all services, to pay homage and to remember the basics of why and what we believe.

I have learned that *Catholic* is not a label, but a faith, and that Catholics are cut from many different fabrics. The church is full of mystics and dogmatics, progressives and conservatives. But we are a community, on our best days united in love.

I was and continue to be drawn to the sacramental life: the love of the Eucharist, the healing of the anointing, the forgiveness I experience through penance. In fact, one of the biggest draws for me to the church was the sacrament of reconciliation. Speaking my sins aloud and hearing forgiveness spoken back to me gives me an unparalleled peace.

At my first confession in the weeks before I was confirmed as a Catholic, I included the sin of disrespect and hurtfulness to my mother that had occurred before my second baptism so many years before, the shame of which I had carried for years. I also confessed my sin of abandoning my family, and so many other transgressions. Saying them out loud made me even sorrier for them. Hearing the priest say, "You are forgiven. Go, and sin no more," made me truly want to live sin free.

At my first communion during the Easter vigil, with my forehead anointed with oil and my body filled with the bread and wine—the body and blood of Jesus—I felt spiritually whole for the first time in my life.

In the years after I received my first communion, my newfound faith was shoved and prodded, in much the same way it had been when I was in my early twenties—but with vastly different results.

Ken's father, Bob, started complaining of various aches and pains, something so atypical of him that finally his wife convinced him to see his doctor. After a few appointments at which the physician had attributed the symptoms to too much yard work, golf, or simply aging, he finally ordered a CT scan. The results showed several areas of Bob's body lit up with activity, signs of advanced cancer.

If you look closely at our wedding photos, you can see that one of Bob's eyes is red and watery, as though infected. But we learned not long after that day that he actually had a rare form of eye cancer. The treatment was aggressive, and at times, brutal, and he eventually lost his eye. But his health since had been stellar. What we hadn't known was that the cancer was still lurking in his body, eventually settling in his bones and causing these mysterious aches and pains.

Once discovered, the disease progressed rapidly. In a single week, Bob went from sitting up in his favorite chair watching his beloved Cincinnati Reds to lying in a bed receiving hospice care, virtually unresponsive.

Ken kept watch with his siblings at the bedside in Dayton. It was a road Ken had walked before, and I knew this inevitable loss would bring back, with fresh pain, the loss he had already experienced. When he called one afternoon, the pain in his voice was so great, I longed to give him some kind of comfort. I pulled Ben, Molly, and Sarah from school and took them to Dayton, knowing they could bring him joy like no one else.

When we got to the hospice center, the girls remained in the hallway with their grandmother, but Ben wanted to see his grandfather, no matter how bad he might feel or look. We walked into the darkened room, where Bob was sitting upright in his bed but seemed unaware of where he was or who was with him.

"Hi, Grandpa," Ben said softly. Bob looked up. And in a rare moment of clarity, he smiled. "Hi, guys," he said, recognizing Ben, so happy to see him.

As we drove back to Columbus that night, I told the kids, "Dad is about to join our special club now, you know."

"The Dead Parent's Club?" Ben asked, recognizing that his father was now on the cusp of losing a parent as he, Molly, Sarah, and I had done years before.

"That's the one," I told him. "The one we'd close membership to if we could. But since we can't, we have to do everything we can to make him comfortable in the club."

Ben was particularly gentle with his dad in the days and weeks after Bob died, giving extra hugs and trying hard to do his chores without being asked—an unlikely feat for a fourteen-year-old boy.

A few months later, life gave us another cruel sucker punch.

Ken's mother, Bev, had been diagnosed with breast cancer the year before Grace was. Ken often looked back at her treatment as a prelude to what would come with Grace. When he put the twins, then age two, to bed at night, he would think, "They are going to grow up not knowing their grandmother." He didn't know then that it would actually be their mother they would have to live without.

Bev's disease stayed at bay, however, until after Bob died. A few months before Bob became sick, the doctors had noticed that the tumor markers in Bev's blood were elevated. After Bob died, the markers spiked, and they encouraged Bev to start chemotherapy. She was reluctant. Losing her husband was excruciating; she battled daily to find meaning in her life, often saying, "I lived with Bob for sixty years. Why couldn't I die with him, too?"

But at her children's urging, she began chemotherapy. Ken took her to one of her treatments. "I think maybe I had a dream," Bev told Ken that day as she sat in a chair hooked up to an IV in a room full of other patients battling the same disease. "Your Dad was sitting on the edge of the bed. He told me it was OK to come with him."

Ken felt her pain, knowing the grief of losing a spouse. "Mom, I think he's just telling you he's OK, and he's in heaven."

But Bev shook her head, unable to explain how real it seemed to her. A day later, she was admitted into the hospital for dehydration, and she died just twelve hours later. The death certificate names cancer as cause of death. The doctors explained that her death was due to complications from the chemotherapy.

But the family knew better. Her death was a testament to Bev's love for her husband. She simply couldn't find another reason to live on this earth if he wasn't here, so she went to live with him in heaven.

It happened so fast we hadn't prepared the children for this newest loss. I told Ken I would break the news to the kids, leaving him to grieve with his siblings and make arrangements for his mother's funeral.

"Grandma's gone, Ben," I told him that morning, standing in the kitchen of his best friend's house the morning after a hastily arranged sleepover. I didn't try to hide the tears on my face.

"No!" he wailed, the sound breaking through the cold gray of the winter morning. He looked at me with anger. "Did you know? Did you and Dad know she was going to die last night?"

"No, Ben," I told him. "I promise you we had no idea."

He collapsed into my arms, and I rocked him, crying with him and shaking my head as he asked over and over, "Why?" I had no answers. I looked heavenward bleakly. Yes, God, why?

Later that day, Father Jeff came over to our house. Ken was still with his siblings. The girls were with friends, away from the sadness. Ben was upstairs. The priest and I stood in the kitchen, the day having already faded into a stone-black night.

"I didn't know what to say to him," I said, recalling the morning. "How do I explain why he lost his mother, now two of his grandparents, too?"

"Use your instincts," Father Jeff said. "You have good instincts."

After we had dinner together, Jeff took Ben into the living room where I could hear them talking. "Are you OK?" the priest asked Ben.

Silence. I could imagine Ben looking down, shrugging.

"Are you mad at God?" Silence, but I knew by the next sentence that Ben had nodded. "That's OK," Jeff said. "It's OK to be mad at God. He can take it. But know that even if we don't understand what's happened, God is here. He's here to take care of us."

I don't know how long Ben was mad at God, but I do know that his grandparents' deaths didn't destroy his faith, any more than his mother's death had. I had evidence to this fact years later, when our roles were reversed.

We were at Mass on a glorious July morning. Ben was a high school junior then, on the varsity tennis team. We were all anxiously waiting to get home to watch an epic battle between Roger Federer and Rafael Nadal at Wimbledon. Those plans crumpled when the priest gave his homily, saying he had just given last rights to a beloved parishioner.

I gasped. We had all known she was dying. We had seen her a few weeks before. Clearly then she was near the end of her battle with melanoma, her frame emaciated, her bald head covered with a knit cap. Yet somehow I had believed that this woman, just a few years older than me, with her bright smile and easy laugh, the woman who first introduced me to yoga and gently chided me when I didn't come to class, would overcome her disease.

So, now, with news that the light of this beacon of joy was indeed going out, I could not draw a full breath. I could barely mouth the words to the profession of faith. I could not even murmur the Our Father. When the priest instructed us to offer one another the sign of peace, I turned to Ben, and my eyes filled with tears. Now a full foot taller than me, he gathered me in his arms and held me tight.

When had he gotten so big, I wondered? When had his faith grown so strong that he could reach out and comfort others, pick them up at the moment they could no longer walk themselves? But I knew the answer. I had watched it for years.

Ben's faith is clear in his voice. He can sing. Not in a singing-in-the-shower or cranking-up-the-tunes in the car kind of way, though he does both. Ben sings in a way that makes people stop and listen. His voice is a gift from his mother. I've heard recordings of Grace singing, and like Ben, it's a sound so blessed and true, it makes the hair on my arms stand up.

Ben is mostly private about his voice these days, but for a while in middle school and then high school he sang more publicly. When he was in seventh grade, St. Brigid put on *Godspell* as its yearly musical. The lead role went to an eighth-grader, but Ben was given a solo, "Beautiful City." It remains one of my favorite songs, and I can't hear it without thinking of him belting it acapella in his deep voice that day in the middle school gym.

In high school, Ben sang in the choir. I think he chose choir at first to get an easy A, but he grew to love the teacher, Mrs. Pritchard. I think, too, that he loved the safe outlet for his talent.

One day when he was a sophomore, I asked him about the upcoming Christmas concert. "What songs are you singing?"

"'O, Holy Night,' the 'Hallelujah Chorus,' and 'Christmas Shoes.'"

I felt the color drain from my face. "Christmas Shoes?" It was a country song, a radio favorite, currently being sung by the Christian group, Newsong. They sang about a little boy wanting to buy shoes for his ill mother before she died, so she could look pretty when she met Jesus. I had never been able to listen to the song without becoming tearful. Since Ben, Molly, and Sarah had come into my life, I turned it off when I heard the first notes—it was too close to reality. Listening to it was like watching the childrens' hearts break over and over.

"I know," Ben said, with a crooked grin.

"But, Ben," I stammered. "I mean, are you OK with that?"

"I think so, yeah. At first it bothered me, but it's just a song now. You know?" If he could be strong, I'd have to be, too.

As the day of the concert got closer, I told him that I wasn't sure I could look at him when he sang it, but I'd try not to cry. "That's OK," he said, smiling. "It's just a song."

The night of the concert, we all filed into the gymnasium. My nephew Josh, six years old now, snuggled next to me. He loved to go to anything that involved Ben, whom he positively adored. I watched Ben intently through the first song, as I always did, trying to make out his voice from all the others.

The first notes of "Christmas Shoes" started, and I steeled myself. About a verse in, I heard a sniffle. The choir sang about the little boy finding shoes just his mother's size.

I heard a little cough.

The choir continued, singing softly about the mother being sick and how she would like the shoes.

Josh began to wail. I wrapped my arms around him, not sure what was happening. "It's just so sad!" he cried.

Suddenly, everyone around me was crying: Ken, my sister, Molly and Sarah, people from the high school who knew the kids and their story. The choir was no longer looking at Mrs. Pritchard, but at the commotion in the stands, yet still singing the sad song. Ben looked at me, and I just shook my head, raising shoulders as though to say, "I didn't see this coming."

Ben threw his head back, laughed, and finished the song, louder and stronger than before. That's when I knew that when it came to death and when it came to faith, Ben was going to be OK.

To this day, when Ben stands next to me at church, I just mouth the words to songs so that I can listen to him sing. I can't doubt God's presence when I hear Ben sing, not just because of the sound itself, but because of where it comes from: a boy, now a man, who lost his mother, two grandparents, and more, but who still sings with joy.

After my confirmation, my own faith began to grow, and apparently it showed.

After Ken and I had been married for two years, Deacon Frank pulled us aside after Mass. "I was wondering if you two would like to be part of our couple-to-couple ministry."

Couple-to-couple paired married couples with couples planning to be married. The married couples served as mentors, helping the to-be-marrieds discern and discuss any potential conflicts before the marriages took place. Before we were married, Ken and I had selected neighbors for our mentor couple. They had been friends to Ken and Grace, and they had a son Ben's age. They were a strong couple and good role models for us. I found the evenings we spent discussing marriage enlightening, before and also after we were married.

But our mentor couple had been married fifteen years. They had history and practice at it. Ken and I had been married just two years. We were essentially still newlyweds.

"I have a couple I'd like to send to you," Frank said. "I think you'd be excellent mentors."

When we received the package of information about the couple, I understood why he had selected us. This couple was older, almost forty. The groom-to-be had only recently converted to Catholicism. Clearly, we had a lot in common with them and were likely to set them at ease, which is crucial to having successful and honest discussions before the marriage.

Not every couple getting married is the typical twenty-something. Many folks fell outside the usual parameters. We often counseled couples who had been married previously and had children from those marriages. We were, by default, experts in blending families.

But with each couple we mentored, my faith—and Ken's and my relationship—grew stronger. Couple-to-couple was a kind of honor, really. This was a ministry for which you could not volunteer; you had to be asked. Couples were selected because they showed signs of having a strong Catholic marriage. From the outside, Ken and I apparently fit that image. And after each encounter with a new couple, after working our way through topics from finances to family to communication, I knew we fit the image inside, too. It helped the other couples be sure they were on the right track; but it helped us, too, working as a reminder as to why we had gotten married in the first place and how, much of the time, we were truly living the sacrament we had taken.

My rediscovered faith is so different now than the faith I had at age twenty-three, the faith I walked away from. When I left San Francisco, I couldn't have predicted that my search was for anything more than simple peace and quiet—that this personal exodus from God was actually the *beginning* of my faith journey.

Despite what I thought I was looking for, this road has been anything but peaceful. Yet the bumps and stumbles no longer make me turn away. I may not have the faith of the proverbial mustard seed, not yet. I'm not exactly moving any mountains. But I've helped form a family—a strong, healthy, faith-filled family. And that is enough.

Roasted Beef Tenderloin with Mushroom Sauce

Makes 8 to 10 servings

A whole roasted beef tenderloin is the ultimate special-occasion meat. I love to make it for our Christmas gatherings because it takes so little time to make (though I usually double the recipe to accommodate the crowd). For smaller family affairs, I cook just the center-cut beef tenderloin (about 2 pounds), which serves the five of us beautifully. The key to this recipe is using the very best beef tenderloin you can find. Try your local butcher shop or ask the meat butcher in your grocery market.

2 tablespoons vegetable oil

1 beef tenderloin (3½ to 4 pounds)

Kosher salt

Ground black pepper

2 tablespoons butter

1 pound brown mushrooms, sliced or quartered

1 small onion, finely chopped

1 teaspoon chopped fresh thyme or ¼ teaspoon dried

½ cup dry red wine

Let meat stand at room temperature for 30 minutes to an hour.

Preheat the oven to 400 degrees.

Heat oil in a large stove-top roasting pan over medium-high heat. Season the beef with salt and pepper. Add to the pan. Cook until browned on all sides, about 8 minutes total.

Transfer pan to oven. Roast, uncovered, until a thermometer inserted in the thickest part registers 125 degrees for medium-rare, about 25 minutes. Transfer the beef to a cutting board. Tent with foil. Let rest 10 to 15 minutes.

While the beef rests, make the sauce. Add the butter to the same roasting pan in which the beef was cooked. Add the mushrooms. Cook over medium-high heat without stirring until the mushrooms brown. Shake the pan and continue cooking until the mushrooms release their liquid and it evaporates, 10 to 15 minutes total. Add onion to the pan. Sauté until tender. Season with salt, pepper, and thyme.

Add the wine to the pan. Bring to a boil, scraping up browned bits. Simmer until the liquid is reduced to a glaze consistency, 5 to 10 minutes.

Slice the beef. Arrange on a platter. Spoon sauce over or serve on the side.

Sautéed Carrots and Parsnips

Makes 8 servings

I like to vary the vegetables I serve at dinner. This recipe is great at big gatherings or at simple family dinners. The kids like the sweetness of the parsnips and the change of pace from the usual carrot sticks they often saw in their packed lunches.

2 tablespoons olive oil

1 pound carrots, cut into 3-by-1-inch sticks

1 pound parsnips, cut into 3-by-1-inch sticks

Kosher salt

Ground black pepper

2 tablespoons butter

1 tablespoon chopped fresh rosemary

1 tablespoon brown sugar or maple syrup

Heat the oil in a heavy large skillet over medium-high heat. Add carrots. Cook 1 to 2 minutes. Add parsnips. Season lightly with salt and pepper. Cook until the vegetables are beginning to brown, 10 to 12 minutes. Add butter, rosemary, and sugar to skillet. Toss over medium heat until glazed. Season with additional salt and pepper if necessary.

7
The Dessert

Good cooks know that when you're creating a special meal, you start with dessert. Sweet finales usually take the longest, and often must be made ahead. Custards such as crème brûlée must be refrigerated to set after baking. Cakes have to cool before they can be frosted and decorated. And some desserts, like pie, are a multistep affair. The crust must be made and chilled before it can be rolled out. The filling must be made, then all of it assembled before it can be baked. And guests still have to wait for the pie to cool before they can eat it.

When Deacon Frank married Ken and me, he told us that the goal of marriage was to get our spouse to heaven. Parenthood carries another goal: to get the kids ready for the world, for life beyond the home.

Most couples wait many years before they have children, let alone think about preparing them to go into the world on their own. For me, parenthood started right away, a necessary ingredient of our marriage. Ken and I immediately worked the dough of the children's lives, filling it with sweet memories, and baking it into a dome of strength and happiness and independence. But, as with making a pie, this multilayered process took lots of practice.

Parents know that the oldest child is the practice child; everything involving that child is, for the parents, new and first. You have no point of reference for the experiences you go through, nothing by which to gauge your child's reactions.

Ben's senior year was rife with stress—for him, and for Ken and me as individuals and as a couple. How much of this stress was related to our hopes and dreams for Ben's future and how much was related to our own inexperience is hard to know.

We started the year by pounding out college applications. I was a strict taskmaster about completing them. I knew that other seniors in years past had spent every free moment of their Thanksgiving and Christmas break completing essays and gathering letters of recommendation.

"That's not going to be you," I told Ben. "All applications will be completed and out of this house by November 1 so you can just enjoy the holidays."

It didn't quite work out that way. Yes, the applications were done by my mandated deadline, out of the house, out of our hair. But right before Christmas, Ben received a rejection letter from one of his top choices.

When I was in high school, Ohio State was everyone's backup school. Everyone applied. Everyone got in. But in the twenty or so years since then, it had become far more competitive.

Ben is a smart boy, but at times he found it tough to apply himself, especially to subjects he didn't like. He wanted good grades (he wanted to please his dad), but he didn't always have the tenacity to work for them. We pushed and cajoled to get him to study more, but Sports Center and Xbox easily distracted him. He ended up with a 3.4 GPA, which is respectable, just not good enough to get into the main campus of Ohio State.

"They just want perfect," Ben ranted. "I heard there are some seniors with 3.8s and 30 on their ACTs who didn't get in." I saw this as a teaching opportunity.

"But that's not you, Ben," I said. "You had a 3.4. You can't really be surprised. It's what we've been saying the past three years. To get the results, you have to do the work."

It was not my finest mothering moment. I may have been right; but my timing, as my mother might have said, "left something to be desired."

Ken quickly stepped in, suggesting that Ohio State probably accepted only a certain number of students from Franklin County because they wanted to be a more diverse school, not just a home-town university. I didn't agree with the tactic. It didn't help much anyway. Ben pouted through the holidays, taking every opportunity to say how much he hated OSU, barely acknowledging the accom-plishment of getting into *all* the other schools to which he applied.

"Robin," Ken said to me later, with grave concern in his voice, "I just think Ben is so fragile right now. I think we need to build him up."

I saw the situation differently. "These are the last few months Ben is going to be living with us. I think it's critical he learns responsi-bility. Cause and effect. I think if we sugarcoat it now, he has a rude awakening next year."

It was a conversation we had already had multiple times. As a freshman, Ben had stopped bringing home his weekly progress reports midwinter. "They just didn't give them out this week," he told us. I bought his explanation the first week, but not the next one.

"You don't believe him?" Ken asked when I brought up my doubts, almost hissing the words at me, letting me know I was on dangerous ground.

When it came to the children, Ken was sometimes blindingly loyal, even turning on me when I presented something he didn't want to see. I, on the other hand, was naturally suspicious, a trait I'd developed after years of working in newsrooms in which every word someone said had to be verified.

But I couldn't drop the issue. I didn't like battling with the kids or my husband, but I didn't believe God had brought me here to be passive in my mothering role.

The next day, I checked with Ben's guidance counselor, who told me that the progress reports were indeed being sent out. Perhaps Ben wasn't sharing them with us, she suggested, because he had a D in English.

We confronted Ben and got him back on track. It was English—Shakespeare even!—something I actually could have helped him with. And we lectured Ben on honesty. Still, there was a rift for a time between Ken and me about my lack of trust in Ben.

It wasn't the only time being the bearer of bad news was a blow to our relationship. Toward the end of the summer after his junior year, I noticed that Ben wasn't working much at his job at the Columbus Zoo. He'd been working concessions at the zoo during the summers since his sophomore year. He hated the job, often working alone at a Dippin' Dot station in the middle of the park or cleaning the grill or the fryer at one of the cafes. He came home hot and sticky, often covered in grease or ice cream.

"You can quit if you find another job," Ken told him.

But when he didn't try to find a new one, we assumed perhaps the job wasn't as bad as Ben had told us. His senior year, we asked him to keep the job during school, too, working one night on the weekend, maybe one night during the week, to build up his bank account for college.

When his hours dwindled, Ken was willing to accept that fall wasn't as busy a time at the zoo and they didn't need as many workers. I was, of course, suspicious. I knew about the big weekends leading up to Halloween and the often record-setting attendance near the holidays, when the zoo is turned into a kind of winter wonderland with elaborate light displays.

When I confessed my doubts to Ken, he responded again with, "Don't you trust him?"

"I just have a feeling maybe Ben isn't telling us the whole truth."

"I have a feeling we need to love and support him."

We later learned that Ben was in fact asking for so many days off that his manager had, in essence, just stopped putting him on the schedule altogether.

"You were right," Ken said, in a tone so biting it could have drawn blood.

I had been right because it was exactly the kind of bonehead move *I* made in high school. When I didn't want to work a shift at McDonald's, I came up with so many tests and drill team practices and sick relatives that they finally stopped putting me on the schedule.

Ben was grounded until he found another job. Unfortunately, I ended up "grounded" with Ken, too, branded the whistle-blower, the messenger bringing bad news.

So that's where we were that December when the rejection letter from OSU came, and when I rather rigidly decided it was a good time to remind Ben that he hadn't studied as much as he should have, and maybe he was at least a little bit responsible for not being accepted.

Years later, after my friend Kristy had a child with her husband Mike, she confided in me. "Being a stepmother is way harder than being a birth mother," she said. "You're always second guessing; there's always someone else with a trump card over your decision. Being a stepmother is harder than anyone knows."

During Ben's senior year, that trump card was in Ken's hands. I knew deep down that Ken's anger wasn't really with me, but the strain between us at times was palpable.

I didn't think any of Ben's behaviors were necessarily unusual for a high school student. They were life lessons with pretty low consequences. After the zoo debacle, he got a job at Montgomery Inn, a sit-down barbecue restaurant, bussing tables. He loved it. He discovered that he liked interacting with people and that the restaurant industry was actually fascinating. And he learned that it's easier to do a good job when it's something you love. He kept the job until he went away to college and occasionally picked up shifts when he was home on break.

Our job, as parents, was just to keep him on the right track, especially in those last few months of high school when it was easy to be distracted. I believed Ben's behaviors were normal. Ken believed they were tied back to grief. He wanted to coddle. I wanted to stand firm.

We were both right.

The transition from high school to college is one of the biggest changes a person goes through, and it starts months before you pack the car to take them to their new home. Each college acceptance—and rejection—comes with a certainty that, come autumn, one way or another, your child's life will no longer be the same.

For Ben, that shift also brought back all the changes that had already been forced upon him. The college application process was yet another reminder that life would continue to go on without his mother, whether he liked it or not.

Were his occasional lapses in judgment all because of grief? That ugly monster no doubt clouded his decisions at times. How much of it was just normal teenage angst and how much of it was mourning? We'll never really know. But I do know that the combination made his senior year particularly challenging to us as parents.

There were, however, some things I did right during Ben's senior year.

He and his date got tossed from a group of kids they had planned on joining for dinner for Cotillion, the winter dance for juniors and seniors. I'm not sure why it happened, but having now watched the girls go through many high school dances, I know the dynamics are fluid and dramatic.

When he told us that he and his date had been booted from their group a week before the dance, I stepped in. "Who are you going to go with?"

"I'm not sure," he said. "We'll get some people together. We have some friends who don't have a group yet."

"Where are you going to go for dinner?" I asked, thinking that at this late date it might be difficult to get reservations for a big group.

"I'm not sure."

"Get a group together and bring them to the Dispatch Kitchen." This was my kitchen space at the North Market, Columbus's public market, where I taped my cooking segments for the local CBS affiliate. It was also ideal for parties. "We'll take pictures there. I'll make dinner, then you'll be closer to the dance anyway."

Ben's mood brightened considerably.

In the end, ten kids and their dates came to the Dispatch Kitchen. Ken, Dorothy, our friends Dwayne and Steve, and Mary, the

Market's marketing director, worked as servers. We passed appetizers for the parents as they took photos, then set one long table for the kids, where I served three courses and had everyone on their way in time for the dance.

As he left with his date, Ben came up and kissed my cheek. "Thank you," he said.

Spring brought tennis. Ben was one of the captains, which made me "tennis mom" by default, along with two other mothers. That meant coordinating transportation to tennis matches and snacks for the team, as well as relaying any messages from the coach to the other parents. Blessedly, the other two mothers who had been coordinators in the past did most of the work.

But the season did mean listening to Ken fret and fume at each match, each stroke, again emphasizing our different approaches: hands on or hands off.

Midseason, Ben was approached by the coach at Otterbein University, a small liberal arts school in a nearby suburb of Columbus. "Have you decided which college you're going to yet?" he asked.

"Not yet," Ben said. He'd been accepted to four universities, but hadn't definitively decided.

Ken took him to visit Otterbein. They toured the school and met the tennis team. It impressed Ben enough that he turned in an application and was quickly accepted.

"Where do you think he'll go?" Ken and I asked each other almost nightly. We knew that tennis was a big draw to Ben, and he was excited to be courted by a coach. He knew it was unlikely that he would make the teams at any of the other schools to which he'd been accepted; he wasn't even planning on trying out. But we all knew that playing sports in college was much different from playing sports in high school; in college it was more of a year-round commitment.

Ken and I secretly hoped Ben would go to the University of Dayton, from which we had both graduated, as had Grace. We had a strong family connection to UD and a strong spiritual connection, too. But we held our thoughts to ourselves, only whispering to each other when the lights were out and we lay in bed.

"Wouldn't it be great . . .?" one of us would say.

"We can't say anything," the other would cut in.

"God will put him where he needs to go," we would agree.

Ben, who was usually forthright in his thoughts and feelings, kept to himself about his college decision, never bringing it up for discussion to either of us.

I came home from work one day and found a yellow piece of paper on the table. It was a form for a graduation banner to put in the front yard.

"Ben, when is this due?" I asked, skimming for a date.

He came in from the dining room. "I'm not sure," he said, with a big smile on his face. "Keep reading."

I scanned the paper more closely. In the line that asked for the inscription on the banner below "Congratulations, Ben" he had written "UD bound."

"Are you sure?" I asked.

"I'm sure. I was sitting in class and it just came to me. I'm going to UD. And I knew that was right."

I jumped up and down and squealed, which was also Ken's reaction when he read the form. In bed that night, when the lights were out, I whispered, "We know where he's going now."

Ken answered, "God put him right where he wants him to be."

Then, suddenly, it was all over. Ben was graduating.

Everything leading up to graduation was like a margarita in a blender: a spinning crushing whirl. We finished tennis, planned for his graduation party—coordinating dates with all the other parties he wanted to attend—and sent out invitations. There was prom and "mom prom" where seniors took their parents to a dance in the gym and rocked out to silly songs of both generations.

On an unusually hot May evening, I found myself at the Baccalaureate Mass, where Ben was to do a reading and then sing with the choir. Sitting in the pew, I felt as if that was the first time I had stopped rushing in weeks. After a few minutes, as I tried to cool myself from the stifling heat by waving the program in front of my face, I could actually breathe.

But instead of feeling relaxed and accomplished, I felt my heart rate start to escalate. Sitting there next to Ken, I realized that in just a few weeks I would be saying good-bye to Ben. It would not be good-bye forever, but it was good-bye to what we now shared and to what we had shared for the past six years. I would no longer be one of the dominant voices in Ben's head. I wouldn't know what he wore, how much he slept, or what television he watched. I would no longer know what he ate or be able to prepare his favorite meals.

His grades were in. He had passed. He was moving on to the next chapter in his life.

What about me? What were my grades in motherhood?

In some ways, Ben had needed me the most. In the beginning, he had needed a mother figure so he wouldn't be different from other kids. I went with him to mother-son dances in the days before he towered over me. I was his partner at the end of the Sunday evening dance classes in the autumn of eighth grade, in which kids learned how to ask someone else to dance and lost some of the awkwardness of social interactions before they got to high school.

Ben had also needed an adult woman to be a positive role model. "This is how women are," my presence told him. And I hoped the message wasn't, "They're crazy. Stay away from women."

Of course, the relationship Ken and I shared was also a kind of lesson for Ben. "This is how a loving married couple acts," we showed him in our day-to-day interactions. And we hoped that the message we gave him was more "marriage is worth the effort" than just "marriage is hard." We hoped and prayed that what Ben saw in Ken and me would help him choose a life partner someday, not scare him away from commitment, as my own parent's relationship had scared me.

So in these final days of full-time stepmotherhood, what was my grade? I had been given less time with Ben—six short years, when most parents were given a full eighteen. As I sat in the church, watching him walk down the aisle to stand at the ambo and read from the book of Peter, I was suddenly overwhelmed. "Wait!" I wanted to cry. "I didn't have him very long! Not even half of his life. I need more time!"

Ben was the first, the experiment, the practice. All of the things I did wrong as a mother, I did with him: obsessing about his hygiene, how clean his room was, and what he ate—holy guacamole, did I obsess about what he ate.

"I need more time!" I bartered. "I need to tell him about love and joy, about it being OK to take chances—but not too many chances—about learning more from your mistakes than from successes, about how winning is not everything."

I wanted to tell him all the things a mother is supposed to know to tell her son. It was suddenly clear that I needed to tell him it wasn't just about eating all your fruits and vegetables and wearing sunscreen. I wanted to tell him that I thought of his mother every day, praying that I might somehow be a good mother to him, though I wasn't sure how well I had listened to what God might have been trying to tell me.

I was panicked. So much to say, so much to tell him.

Then I looked at the people around me. All eyes were on Ben, the confident young man, reading from the ambo. "You are a chosen people, a royal priesthood, a holy nation, a people belonging to God, that you may declare the praises of him who called you out of darkness into his wonderful light," he read clearly and precisely in his baritone voice. "Once you were not a people, but now you are the people of God; once you had not received mercy, but now you have received mercy."

There was not a sound in the church packed with 1,000 students, parents, and teachers. Everyone was looking at Ben.

I watched as he closed the lectionary, walked to the front of the altar, and bowed. I saw him nod respectfully to the bishop who was presiding over the Mass, then walk to the choir loft to sing with that voice God had given him.

I stole glances at him during Mass, as he sang, as he took communion. I watched the joy on his face as he hugged his friends afterwards.

Robin, I thought, *he knows. All the things you want to tell him, he already knows.*

I'm not sure I'm the one who taught him. And heaven knows I could have used some editing in the delivery of any life lessons I administered. But as I watched him that night, and in the days following his graduation—at his party and weeks later when we packed him up to go to the University of Dayton—I realized that if grades were given for motherhood, I had passed. Ben was a fully functioning, handsome, smart, God-loving, kind young man. Despite wounds to his heart at such an early age, despite being given an inexperienced stepmom who stumbled more than she flew, he had turned out just fine.

Maybe my mothering report card wouldn't show an A+, but I've finally stopped believing that A+ moms actually exist. We all have our flaws, our shortfalls.

But if Ben's graduation was also my graduation, I, too, was ready for the next chapter. As this gift, which Grace had entrusted to me, got his high school diploma, so I received my diploma of sorts.

At Grace's funeral, Ken talked about her entering a new life, her eternal life. After Ken and I met, friends and family often marveled at how Ken also had been given a new life when I walked into his world.

In reality, though, I was the one who received new life. Grace had run her race, fought her battle, and now lived victorious with her reward in heaven. Ken, truth be told, would have succeeded as a father, a complete person, if he'd never met me. He had the kind of faith that was going to help him persevere and endure.

What did I have?

Until I met Ken, Ben, Molly, and Sarah, I was lacking something; I was empty. By saying yes to God's calling despite my fears, by diving into a life for which I felt so unprepared, by accepting the love of my husband and his children, and by being no one other than who I was at my core, I was reborn, complete, and finally, whole.

Sour Cherry Lattice Pie

Makes 8 servings

My mother used to say that the skill for making piecrust skipped generations. It had skipped her, so I must be the pie maker, she said. It was true that she made dreadful piecrust—it was one of the very few things she couldn't make. I first learned to make piecrust in an adult extension class in San Diego long before I went to cooking school. But years in various test kitchens taught me that the trick to good crust is gentleness.

For all the practice it took me—and takes most cooks—pie making came naturally to Ken. One summer day we snagged a bunch of sour cherries at a farmer's market. He told me he was going to make a lattice-crust pie, from scratch, all by himself. And he did. Perfectly. He used my recipe but asked for no help. I have pretty much turned all pie-making responsibilities over to him.

If you can't find cherries, you can use any berry: blackberries, raspberries, or strawberries. Adjust the sugar and lemon juice in the filling according to how sweet the berries taste.

Crust:

2⅔ cups flour

2 tablespoons sugar

½ teaspoon salt

1 cup chilled unsalted butter, cut into small pieces

½ cup ice water

Filling:

1 cup sugar

3 tablespoons cornstarch

½ teaspoon salt

6 cups pitted sour cherries or sweet cherries

1 teaspoon fresh lemon juice if using sour cherries or 3 tablespoons if using sweet cherries

½ teaspoon almond extract (optional)

Milk for brushing

Coarse sugar or additional granulated sugar for sprinkling

To make crust: Combine flour, sugar, and salt in a food processor. Using on/off turns, cut in the butter until mixture resembles coarse meal, with a few pea-sized pieces. Add water. Process until moist clumps form. If dough is dry, add more water by teaspoonful, just until it holds together.

Divide dough in half. Form each into a disk. Wrap in plastic and refrigerate at least 1 hour or up to 3 days ahead. Let dough soften slightly at room temperature before rolling.

Position rack in lower third of oven and preheat oven to 400 degrees.

Roll out 1 dough disk on lightly floured surface to a 12-inch round. Transfer to a 9-inch glass pie dish. Carefully fit crust into dish. Trim crust even with dish.

Combine sugar, cornstarch, and salt. Add cherries, lemon juice, and extract (if using). Toss to coat. Fill bottom crust with cherry mixture.

Roll out second dough disk to 12-inch round. Using a pastry wheel or knife, cut 10 strips, each ½-inch wide. Place 5 strips in one direction over the cherry filling and 5 strips in the opposite direction, forming lattice. Press strips into edge of crust to seal. Trim any overhang. Crimp edges.

Brush crust with milk. Sprinkle with coarse sugar or additional granulated sugar. Place dish on baking sheet.

Bake 15 minutes. Reduce oven temperature to 375 degrees. Bake until crust is golden brown and filling is bubbling, about 1 hour longer, covering edge of pie if it browns too quickly.

Postscript
Coffee and Tea

At the end of a celebratory meal, after the plates and cutlery have been whisked away, cups of steaming coffee and tea remain. The postmeal drink gives folks the chance to digest both the food and the events that brought them together. Guests linger, shoes off, any formality gone, just taking the time to tell stories and spend a few more minutes in one another's company.

The house is quiet most days now; but if I listen closely, I can hear young voices and laughter. I catch shadows of Ben, Molly, and Sarah running through the rooms or sitting around the kitchen table. They are so much a part of the space that sometimes I still set places for five at dinner, forgetting that our young adults no longer live here.

Ben is in his third year at the University of Dayton, studying business and working with the athletic department at sporting events. He is a true Dayton Flyer, through and through, with a collection of UD T-shirts he would wear proudly every day if he could.

He's long since gotten over his disappointment of not being accepted to Ohio State's main campus, though he confided in me not too long ago that he would have had a tough time deciding between UD and OSU if he had been accepted. It's hard to imagine him on the OSU campus, though, and how different his life would have been there.

Ben didn't come home this past summer, instead taking a marketing internship with the Dayton Dragons, the Cincinnati Reds' farm club. We knew it would happen eventually. It's crucial for students to get internships in their field of choice to increase their job prospects. Still, it was unsettling for us to see him only a few weekends during the summer. At the same time, we were busy getting Molly and Sarah ready to leave for college, so we filled that emptiness with a whirl of activity.

Moving girls to college, we learned, was more complicated than moving a boy. Girls seem to have more stuff. And moving two girls to different colleges doubled the effort.

Molly chose to follow her brother—and parents, stepmother, and a host of aunts, uncles, and cousins—to the University of Dayton. At Ken's suggestion, she took up engineering as her major.

"You just think like an engineer," he told her one night at dinner, pointing out her meticulous methods for studying and her penchant for math and science. When she told us she was most excited about her calculus class after she'd been at college just a few weeks, we knew she was on the right track.

Sarah held on to the idea of dancing as a major until after her first round of auditions during the fall of her senior year. When they proved more brutal than she had anticipated, she regrouped and chose to focus on nursing instead. In the depth of her soul, Sarah is a caretaker. Watching her babysit or teach dance to young children convinced us that she needed to incorporate her giving nature into her career.

When we were arranging college visits her junior year, I suggested Loyola University in Chicago. It was one of the few schools that offered both nursing and dance. She lit up during that visit in a way she didn't at any other school she saw, even her top dance choices. God has a way of working things out just as they should. Sarah is majoring in nursing with a dance minor at Loyola, the school where, I believe, she always belonged.

Of course, because of the girls' interests, we knew long ago that they wouldn't be attending the same school. None of the schools Molly applied to had nursing or dance; none of Sarah's schools had engineering. So part of our challenge during the summer before their first semester was helping these twins say good-bye to each other. Molly and Sarah are very different, in looks and personality, but at the end of the day, they're best friends, too. They're now in the process of redefining that friendship while they live hundreds of miles apart in new, exciting, and quite separate worlds.

Now Ken and I are trying to establish adult—and separate—relationships with the children. I check in mostly via texts throughout the week, innocuous questions about what they're eating and who they're with. Ken does the same on his own schedule, asking about course work. We try to talk to the kids individually or together by phone or Skype at least once a week.

Ken and I are in a new world of our own, too. We have never been together without kids in our eight years of marriage, save a few nights here and there. I like to say we are in a reverse marriage, having our honeymoon after a decade together. Most couples at this stage are returning to what they had at the beginning of their marriage. We didn't have a beginning. Just a middle.

Of course, it's not really like a honeymoon, a true period of discovery. We had that in the midst of parenting. We're now in more of an adjustment period, one that is particularly hard on Ken at times.

When Grace was dying, Ken promised her that he and the kids would be OK. He devoted his life to making it so. The first year Ben was gone to college and then the next year, the girls' senior year, Ken struggled with the thought of their leaving. With all of his children gone, so was his life's purpose.

But God calls each of us to keep moving forward. Ken's sister, Kim, has a magnet in her office that I think of often. It says, "Faith doesn't make life easy. Just possible."

As solace for so much grief, Ken was given the gift of a new life partner, someone to hold his hand and wipe his tears and with whom to move to the next chapter with him, once the children were grown.

The children's leaving was, in some ways, easier for me. I'd made big life-altering changes throughout my adult life: moving from coast-to-coast, changing careers, and changing jobs within those careers. It was, after all, one of those complete changes in direction that brought me to Ken, Ben, Molly, and Sarah.

But to say I eased into a childless life unscathed isn't true. I may like that the house looks the same when I get up in the morning as when I went to bed the night before: no shoes in the doorway, no dishes on the counter or in the sink. And it's easier to put a meal on the table for two than for five. But I'm conscious of the echoes of the empty house and the life that has left it. It's quiet in a way that makes me wonder how I ever lived happily all alone.

Ken and I are redefining our own routines. We're free to attend any Mass now, not having to wait for the kids to wake up. We usually go to earlier ones than we used to, avoiding the later and more crowded Masses filled with school-age children and families. We often drive to work together, and we can decide to grab a bite at a new restaurant on a whim without having to worry about what the kids will eat or who might need a car.

While parenting is never really over, we both have the sense that we've closed a chapter, completed this particular journey God set before us. Part of the comfort we can give each other is pointing out how well we handled this calling. Despite the challenges, which were often great, we managed to turn out three strong, faith-filled young adults who are now adapting well to their new lives. Ken and I can humbly say to each other with true humility, "Job well done."

Mostly we're just enjoying each other's company, marveling in the blessings of having this life and love to share together.

At the orientation Mass at UD the day we left Molly to start her freshman year, the priest asked us to place our hands on the students we were about to leave behind and to repeat a prayer after him, with the last words being, "You are loved."

As the moms and dads sniffled their good-byes before heading away, I realized that the words were for us, too. *We* are loved. By our families and by our children, yes. But loved also by God, who whispered into our hearts before we were born and continues to whisper throughout each chapter of our lives: "You are loved."

And with that love, anything is possible.

Acknowledgments

"My Lord God, I have no idea where I'm going. I do not see the road ahead of me. I cannot know for certain where it will end. Nor do I really know myself, and the fact that I think I am following Your will does not mean that I am actually doing so. But I believe that the desire to please You does in fact please You. And I hope I have that desire in all that I am doing."

—Thomas Merton, *Dialogues with Silence*

When Ken and I would hit a particularly difficult path in our lives, we would say to each other how we wished there was a book, a road map to our circumstances, proof that other people had traveled the sometimes bumpy road we found ourselves on. Years later it became clear that there could be such a book if I would write it. And so I did.

The stories in this book are true as I remember them, though I did consolidate some parts out of respect for those people whose lives intersected with mine, but who preferred I not include them specifically.

I owe my thanks to many people for helping me tell this story: my agent, Jennifer, who patiently helped me grow the idea so completely into what it became. To Kim, who didn't let me fool myself into believing a broken hard drive was a sign I should stop writing, but was only a sign that I needed a new computer. To the people at

Loyola Press, especially Joe, who saw the potential of the story and wanted it told, and to Vinita, who helped me make all the edits, especially the hard ones.

But mostly to Ben, Molly, and Sarah, who told me what they remembered and bravely read what I wrote. Your acceptance of me in your lives is one of the most concrete pieces of evidence I have of God's grace.

And to Ken, who through everything is my rock and my pillow, whose fearlessness and selflessness inspire me every day.

About the Author

Robin Davis has been a food writer for almost 20 years. She is currently the food editor at the *Columbus Dispatch*, where she hosts a weekly cooking segment on the local CBS affiliate. She is a wife to Ken and stepmother to Ben, Molly, and Sarah.

Also Available

Random MOMents of Grace
Experiencing God in the
Adventures of Motherhood
$13.95 • Pb • 3840-6

In *Random MOMents
of Grace,* Moyer helps
mothers realize that their
spiritual lives don't have to
stagnate even though most
of their time is now spent
in a world of play dates and
playgrounds. In fact, Moyer
contends that all that wiping of noses and reading of bedtime
stories can lead to some pretty amazing spiritual growth.

For any mom wondering if it's possible to be fully engaged in
the lives of her children without sacrificing her spirituality,
Random MOMents of Grace offers a definitive "yes" as
it shows moms how to see God's grace at work in even
the silliest, messiest, and most frustrating moments of
motherhood.

To order: call 800-621-1008,
visit www.loyolapress.com/store,
or visit your local bookseller.

Also Available

Love & Salt
A Spiritual Friendship Shared in Letters

$14.95 • Pb • 3831-4

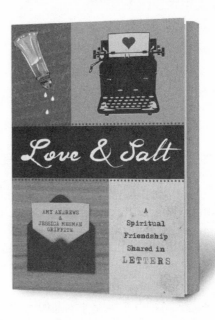

After a chance meeting in a creative writing class, and inspired by the unlikely friendship of Ruth and Naomi in the Old Testament, Amy Andrews and Jessica Mesman Griffith embark on a lifelong friendship, but one separated by distance and time.

They decide to write letters to each other—at first, for each day of Lent, but those days extend into years. Their letters became a memoir in real time and reveal deeply personal and profound accounts of conversion, motherhood, and crushing tragedy.

Told through the timeless medium of letters—in prose that is raw and intimate, humorous, and poetic—*Love & Salt* is at its core the emotional struggle of how one spiritual friendship is formed and tested in tragedy, tempered and proven in hope.

Also Available

Thrift Store Saints
Meeting Jesus 25¢ at a Time

$13.95 • Pb • 3301-2

Thrift Store Saints is a collection of true stories based on Jane Knuth's experiences serving the poor at a St. Vincent de Paul thrift store in the inner city of Kalamazoo, Michigan. At the outset of the book, Knuth is a reluctant new volunteer at the store, sharing that her middle-class, suburban, church-going background has not prepared her well for this kind of work. By the end of the book, Knuth has undergone a transformation of sorts, and neither she nor we can ever view the poor in the same way again.

Thrift Store Graces
Finding God's Gifts in the Midst of the Mess

$13.95 • Pb • 3692-1

In *Thrift Store Graces*, Knuth introduces us to some far more challenging personal situations that emerge as a result of her volunteer work—where she learns that when we help the poor, they end up helping us. Additionally, she invites us to join her as she hesitantly embarks on a pilgrimage to Medjugorje in war-torn Bosnia. Through it all, her delightful sense of humor keeps her going, along with her conviction that some of God's greatest gifts come disguised as difficulties.

Continue the Conversation

If you enjoyed this book, then connect with Loyola Press
to continue the conversation, engage with other readers,
and find out about new and upcoming books from your
favorite spiritual writers.

Visit us at
www.LoyolaPress.com
to create an account
and register for our
newsletters.

Or you can just click on the code to the
right with your smartphone to sign up.

Connect with us on the following:

Facebook   **Twitter**   **You Tube**
facebook.com/loyolapress   twitter.com/loyolapress   youtube.com/loyolapress